GATHER US IN

Leading Transformational Small Groups

ANGELA D. SCHAFFNER

UPPER ROOM BOOKS®
NASHVILLE

Cover Design: Jay Smith, Juicebox Designs

Cover photo: Daly and Newton

Interior design and typesetting: PerfecType | Nashville, TN

ISBN (print): 978-0-8358-1943-5 | ISBN (mobi): 978-0-8358-1944-2
ISBN (epub): 978-0-8358-1945-9

Printed in the United States of America

For Erin Palmer

CONTENTS

ACKNOWLEDGMENTS

I thank God for the opportunity to write and for the transformational relationships I've encountered. I extend deep gratitude to all of my friends, family members, and clients who tell me their truths even when it's difficult. And I thank every person with whom I've sat in a group, side-by-side, declaring vulnerable hard truths and listening to the truths of others. The Bible studies I attended and led while I spent time at Miami University, Judson College, University of Illinois, Ball State University, Oak Grove United Methodist Church, and in my one-of-a-kind Leafmore neighborhood helped me know God better through the hearts, lives, and wisdom of the people in these groups. My own therapy groups at Rapha, Miami University Counseling Center, and Pine River Psychotherapy propelled my self-awareness at an intense but healing pace that left a lasting impression. The group therapy I provided for clients during my training at Ball State, my internship at Emory University Counseling Center, and on staff at Atlanta Center for Eating Disorders shaped my view of therapy and change. My book club, my Taekwondo community, and my Leafmore neighborhood friends provide ongoing insight and support. I witness unforgettable transformations again and again in these groups.

My editor, Erin Palmer, invested care and attention to detail, offered honest personal reflections, and employed her expertise in powerful ways during the creation of *Revealed* and *Gather*

Us In. She shaped my writing into something deeper and more whole through *Revealed* and gave me courage to keep writing. Through an initial conversation with her, the idea for *Gather Us In* was born. She held my stories in her hands and treated them with the utmost respect, and I'm so grateful. Joanna, Erin, and the whole team at Upper Room Books turned my ideas and manuscripts into actual books that people are now buying, asking me to sign, and taking on their beach vacations. Thanks to them, my dream came true!

Jaime Blandino has stood by me through over fifteen years of friendship and generously extends warmth, love, and astoundingly radical acceptance of me. There's no part of me that hasn't been touched by bringing my writing from my computer and journals out into the world, and Jaime helped me navigate the necessary emotional overhaul involved with grace, patience, and wisdom.

Camber, Michelle, Nyree, Kelly, and Elaine bring out my most honest and unfiltered self, whether we are riding on an inflated banana in the Caribbean, sharing a meal and drinks, immersing ourselves in a silent disco experience, running a 5K, or exchanging colorful texts. Before these friends entered my life, my name was always just "Angela" when I went bowling. These friends offer a soft landing place when life gets hard, remind me that I am loved, and demonstrate courage to speak the truth always.

Danielle Veader's generosity and kindness make our friendship a constant comfort to me. She is grounded in faith, and her emotional stability steadies me. She and I share a silent understanding about so many things. And the things that need to be spoken will always fall within her capacity for both embracing people fully and maintaining an unwavering faith.

Michelle O'Donnell is the best companion on a Friday night after a trying week. She won't tolerate my negative self-talk and has my back constantly. She generously shares her food, wine, and guest room with me while also somehow convincing me that I don't owe her anything. Her rational voice of practicality and intolerance for the oppressive voices in our lives is always a soothing remedy.

Susan Allen Grady's balanced wisdom and grounded presence offers calm, still waters amid even the most anxiety-producing circumstances. Her strength, resilience, and ability to continue ministering to others with consistency, balance, and love is downright impressive. I will keep striving to emulate those qualities that she lives out so well.

My sons Carlson, Caleb, and Zach bring joy to me on a daily basis. During this season of their childhoods, I've especially enjoyed Carlson's sense of humor and expanding self-awareness, Caleb's sensitivity and self-expression, and Zach's laughter and affection.

Mom, Dad, Elise, Karen, Terry, and Erin continue to love and support me, making time for meals and visits together and time with our boys. To my knowledge, my mother-in-law, Karen, has hands down bought the most copies of *Revealed*, and that means the world to me!

Dusty offered insightful feedback and unwavering support of my writing as my partner and coleader for over twenty years. Our relationship continues to evolve as we grow and change, stand as witnesses and advocates for one another, and make space for each other's difficult questions, uncertainty, and silence. Our family is a small group, and we are the co-facilitators. We begin and end our very full days together, work out the surprises and complexities, process what we know and what we have yet to learn, and seek to embrace the most challenging questions with integrity and courage. We are in it together for life, and we will keep celebrating our love as we go.

Introduction

One hundred Presbyterian retreat attendees stood in the auditorium and assumed a Taekwondo fighting stance. We were all on a retreat in Montreat, North Carolina, and I coached them to give their loudest *kihap*, a yell that is done along with a strike or kick in Taekwondo. The entire group practiced a hammer fist strike into the air and gave their loudest yell, and the energy in the room increased tenfold as a highly intellectual, analytical, and self-reflective group of people moved collectively into their bodies and allowed their emotions to surface. Mind, body, and spirit came together in a moment that powerfully connected us. We witnessed an important gift offered to the church by psychology: the integration of the emotional self into the faith journey. The wise mind that God ushers us into when we make space for both intellect and emotion yields a wise faith that celebrates the whole person. That kind of faith means that the church can become a place people want to run *to* instead of *from* during times of suffering. We need a church we can run to now more than ever.

My first book, *Revealed: What the Bible Can Teach You About Yourself*, includes deeply personal stories from my life. I notice a particular look in the eyes of people who have read it. In the dark of an early morning, a neighbor and mother of two young children looked at me that way after our children got on the bus. She remarked lovingly that she could tell that I'd put my heart and soul into *Revealed*. A retired Methodist minister answered the door one evening when his wife was hosting a book club where I'd come to talk about *Revealed*, and he gave me the same look. I began to see that look in more and more peoples' eyes. It also happened after I led workshops on *Revealed*. I recognize in hindsight others who have looked at me that way since reading the book. Was it a sense of appreciation? A look of seeing me for who I am? A type of admiration? It was difficult to pinpoint. The look seems to have some emotion to it—a sense of having held my stories in their hands—communicating an appreciation of how difficult it was for me to put my stories into words and release them into others' lives. I've come to understand that look as a gift people give me in exchange for my stories. It is a sense of being seen and valued. Their intimate interactions with my stories build a sense of connection between us.

A deeper connection is possible through ongoing interaction, as we sit together in a small group and study scripture, share a meal, and listen to one another's stories and experiences. Small groups provide one route from an initial, meaningful connection to an experience of emotional and spiritual transformation. As a psychologist, I want to be a catalyst for change, helping people navigate their relationships with greater self-awareness, skill, and self-respect in order to experience transformation. We can all experience transformation through our relationships with one another. We simply need to create an opportunity for a connection and may need a little help facilitating transformation. Small groups can provide us with the space for meaningful connection within the church, and this book will help you know how to facilitate connections that can be transformative.

Even in spiritually thriving congregations, emotional and relational problems are rampant. In over twenty years of participating in and leading small groups, I cannot count the number of hours I've voiced and listened to emotionally oriented prayer requests stemming from some sort of relational dispute, mental health diagnosis, or unsettling sense of uncertainty. One person prays for her best friend's divorce and child custody proceedings. Another prays for her son's anxiety and her long-term unresolved tensions with parents and siblings. Another prays for her uncertainty about which teacher, school, coach, tutor, or therapist will be the right fit for her child. Another person raises concerns about conflict with a coworker, about a friend who seems withdrawn and depressed, and about a member of the community whose child died by suicide. We are surrounded by relational struggle, and we are looking for relational healing.

As leaders of small groups, we have an opportunity to offer an environment for relational healing where there have been relational wounds. While relational healing may feel like a big responsibility, it is also doable. We can make space for authentic, positive connections between group members. Anyone who is willing to do some basic self-examination and learn a few important skills and tools can fill this role. Facilitating transformational relationships is more about setting a tone of curiosity and persevering than about having biblical training, more about asking questions than having answers, and more about being vulnerable and honest about faith than about being a fault-free role model.

Leading a small group does not have to be the Goliath task that some fear it to be as long as, like David, we are equipped with a slingshot, some stones, and our faith in God. I'll begin by dispelling some of the common myths about leading small groups and why leading one is much more doable than we may think. Our slingshot will be a general understanding of how groups work as living systems with stages, explained throughout section 1 of the book. I'll describe eleven group dynamics that result in positive changes for group members and explain how and why we can have a powerful group experience by focusing on what is happening in the moment and by creating the opportunity for transformational emotional and spiritual experiences for others. Our stones will be the eight strategies in section 2, described in detail and designed to provide us with applicable tools you can use right away.

Equipped with your slingshot and just a few stones, you can conquer the Goliath challenges within yourself that stand in the way of leading well. You can move forward into the space you'd like to occupy as a leader. If you're a busy and tired leader who at best skims books, you can find a short action checklist at the end of each chapter in section 2. If that's your preference, you can go back and read about just the topics where you feel you need more direction. This book is meant to be an easy-to-use reference to help you feel more equipped to lead a small group. This book is not meant to overwhelm you with too much information. That's why we will begin with some surprising news: You probably already know more than you think you do about leading groups just by being a person who lives in this world and notices what you experience with other people.

For simplicity and consistency's sake, I will use the term *small group* throughout the book, but you may prefer the terms *Bible study, covenant group,* or *book club.* The tools and strategies I describe in this book apply to all of the above.

Your faith in God is a critical component in this endeavor. God's been in God's own small group of three from the beginning. God is plural in the creation story, in communion with Jesus and the Holy Spirit. (See Genesis 1:26.) Your group is engaging in a creative process too. You'll work to separate light from darkness; witness, name, and care for new life; and find collective rest amid your group's creative journey. The best creations and outcomes are a result of the mysterious flow that pulses through the relational power of community and transcends what an individual can experience and accomplish.

The Holy Spirit is present as our primary group facilitator, guiding the body of Christ, if we only will allow room for the Spirit to move and prompt us along. The Holy Spirit is present in and among believers as a unifying and influential facilitator of faith. The Spirit leads us toward truth by guiding us gently in directions that speak to our hearts on deeply individual levels and by uniting us in central truths as believers in Christ.

God gives us encounters more than God gives us people. Other people do not belong to us like possessions, and we need to treat others with respect for their autonomy. We also encounter parts of ourselves through our interpersonal encounters. Other people have a way of drawing attention to parts of ourselves that we may or may not feel ready to encounter. We encounter God and carry the spiritually transforming experiences God gives us into our relationships with ourselves and other people. Our everyday interactions continue to shape our relational selves. It can be useful entering into a group study to reflect upon three questions regarding the encounters in our lives:

1. How am I encountering God?
2. How am I encountering myself?
3. How am I encountering others?

Ask these questions as a regular reflection before or after your group. Keep a journal that you use just for your small group to record your reflections about these questions and other insights and ideas throughout the course of the group.

Soon we will move on to what you need to know for understanding how groups work and the tools and strategies you can use to facilitate a small group that leads group members to spiritual and emotional maturity. But first, let's dispel a few common myths about leading small groups.

Myths About Leading

Leading a small group requires a basic skill set that anyone can develop. Leadership comes more naturally to some, but it is not impossible for anyone. This section will help you identify and dispel some common myths about what it takes to lead a small group and increase your confidence in being an effective leader.

Myth 1: I would need special training in interpreting the Bible.

After I wrote *Revealed,* several people told me that they liked my exegesis. I googled *exegesis* (it means interpretation or explanation) and realized this was a great compliment. With the reassurance of people who have multiple Bible degrees, I got through my doubt and imposter phenomenon and learned that I could read and interpret scripture in a helpful way, even without extensive seminary training. We are all on a journey together of interpreting the Bible, and there are varying perspectives and plenty of topics to discuss with just about any passage of the Bible you choose to read and examine in a group context. You can use a study Bible that has added notes and references in the Bible itself. I am grateful for the many excellent guides and commentaries on the Bible written by people who do have seminary degrees. There are books that come with facilitator guides that essentially provide you with all of the content you need for a group study.[1] You're not in this alone. Don't hesitate to reach out to your church's groups leader or pastor to help you identify potential studies and resources. You do not need to know all the answers to have an effective group. One of the major tasks of a small group is exploring the questions together.

Myth 2: I must pray aloud in eloquent spiritual language.

I've met more than a few people who fear praying aloud. People seem to pray with a different sort of language and in a different way of speaking that can sound extensively practiced and unfamiliar to listeners. Those who fear praying aloud are often excellent, capable leaders who weren't raised in the church, who view prayer as more of a private than a shared experience, or who simply aren't comfortable praying aloud. There is absolutely nothing wrong with this. In fact, while I suggest making prayer a part of the group time in some way, there is certainly nothing wrong with reading a psalm as prayer, inviting a group member to close in prayer, making a list of prayer requests and emailing them out to group members for personal prayer during the week, or writing a prayer to send with the group each week. One Sunday school class I recently visited passes around a notebook for group members to record prayer requests, and then the leader emails them to everyone after class.

Myth 3: I've never led a group before, so I cannot lead a small group.

There is no shortcut to gaining experience. Give group-leading a try. You will learn something, even if you learn that you do not want to lead another group. A fellow psychologist said to me once that if you're not failing at something, you're not taking enough risks. We almost always learn valuable lessons when we step out of our comfort zone.

Myth 4: Leading groups is not my spiritual gift.

Leading involves a set of skills that may come more naturally to some but can be developed by others with some practice and guidance. Introverts and extroverts can both lead groups. Salespersons and computer programmers can both lead groups. People with any variety of spiritual gifts will lead groups differently but not necessarily better or worse. Remember that part of leading a group is leading in an authentic way that expresses your unique reflection and identity in the beautifully diverse body of Christ. There is not one right way to lead. Effective tools can help any type of person become a stronger leader, and you'll learn them in this book.

Myth 5: Something about leading a group will be uncomfortable for me, so I should avoid doing it.

Embracing honesty and vulnerability, letting go of perfection, and stepping forward in courage and faith allow people to lead well. Avoiding opportunities for maturity and change only keeps us on a plateau, in a state of spiritual stagnancy. The leader role is doable for any Christian who is committed to faith, willing to be in authentic relationships, and equipped with some knowledge about how people function within a group, which this book provides. When we learn to sit with some discomfort, we can grow in faith.

Myth 6: I will need a lot of time to prepare for leading a group every week. Between time to prepare and the time and energy needed to lead the group itself, I don't have time in my life for it.

With all the excellent studies and facilitator guides available, you can prepare in as little as fifteen to thirty minutes plus whatever reading is required for that week. You likely already spend that much time on a leisure activity that could stand to be postponed or lessened. If you host the meeting at your home, preparing the space may be the most difficult part; but you don't have to host it at your home. Many groups meet in coffee shops, pubs, churches, or other locations. I have done therapy groups outdoors in a wooded area at a picnic table. I've facilitated groups over Skype. And I have led meaningful, fulfilling groups while balancing multiple roles in my career and nursing babies through the night. No matter how busy you are, you really can do this. In fact, the busier you are, the more you may need the relationally interdependent, spiritually nourishing type of life that a group offers.

Myth 7: Leading a small group is not my thing and is uniquely difficult. Who do I think I am, some kind of pastor or seminary student?

You do not have to have a lot of spiritual training to lead a group that is spiritual in nature. The only real difference between small groups and other conversations in groups of friends is the intentional effort to focus the discussion on God and to pray together. Your faith journey and your desire to create space for transformational relationships equips you to be a leader. This book will give you the knowledge and tools to lead with confidence.

Section 1

Do What Works in Groups

Enter the System

If one member suffers, all suffer together with it; if one member is honored, all rejoice together with it.

—1 CORINTHIANS 12:26

Groups honor the great commandment to love neighbor as self, a relational calling to every believer. (See Matthew 22:39.) None of us is exempt from the call to be in relationships—even introverts who need a lot of down time; even people who don't like forced fun in the form of icebreakers; even people who need things to be ordered and predictable. We all are included in God's call to love one another, and fulfilling that call requires interaction.

A central defining characteristic of a group is that its members are interdependent as they work to accomplish a task or benefit in social or emotional ways. In small groups we seek spiritual maturity at the same time. Paul emphasizes the picture of interdependence in the body of Christ, where we cannot all be an eye or an ear, but we need eyes and ears to function at our full potential. (See 1 Corinthians 12:12-26.)

Groups are considered living systems.[1] The first system we know is the one in which we are raised, our family of origin. Our primary caregivers, whoever was in the home where we grew up on a regular basis, played a major role in shaping who we are and how we cope with life. In our families of origin, we learn to adopt roles such as the peacemaker, the instigator of conflict, the decision-maker, the challenger, or the quiet but attentive observer. We learn and adapt to roles determined by our environment, personality, and preferences. We tend to adopt the same types of roles later when we enter different systems, including classrooms, teams, work places, and—you guessed it—small groups.

Since a group is considered a living system, you may want to enter the system you are leading with some self-awareness of how you've approached other systems in your life. Your family of origin is a good example. Take a moment to reflect on the role you played within your family as a young child, as an adolescent, and later on as an adult child. Do members of your family come to you for help? Do you engage in conflict readily or tend to avoid conflict? Do you serve as a go-between when two family members aren't getting along? Do you fly quietly below the radar and steer clear of drama? You know systems beyond your family of origin too. You may have participated in sports' teams, choirs, committees, Bible studies, and various friend groups. You've probably worked on a group project or two. Did you lead and delegate, follow someone else's lead, divide the work evenly, or do it all yourself? Because of your existing experiences in systems, you already know some things about being in groups and have ideas about what leadership choices work and don't work.

Take some time now to reflect on what you already know. Do you readily step into a leadership role when no one else steps up, figuring things out as you go? Or do you tend to be more comfortable when there is a structured plan to follow

ENTER THE SYSTEM

as a leader? Do you generally like larger groups or smaller
groups? If you attended college, were you drawn to a smaller
college or large university? Did you enjoy some anonymity in
big lecture halls, or did you prefer smaller classes where the
professor knew you by name and noticed if you were absent? In
job settings, do you gravitate toward roles where you can present, entertain, or talk in front of people? Do you like working
independently or on a team? Are you a "behind the scenes"
person? Do you want and need recognition and affirmation
for your work? Do you like a lot of socializing or prefer to work
in a quiet setting and have ample downtime? Your answers to
these questions provide a helpful context as you prepare to
lead your small group.

   As you note the groups you've been a part of and the lessons
learned in each, bring to mind what you already know based
on your experience. For instance, through leading meal and
therapy groups with clients who have eating disorders, I know
the value of letting people take on challenges at their own pace
and not overwhelming anyone with too much feedback all at
once. Through exposure to family members with intense anxiety, I know how to provide a calming presence and have learned
to set healthy boundaries and recognize when I begin to take
on and absorb too much of others' anxious tendencies. I now
know it is not my job to fix another adult's anxiety but simply to
make space for it and provide loving support. Make a list of the
groups in which you have taken part; next to each, write down
what you learned about yourself and others. You'll see that you
already come to this process equipped with some knowledge
that will be useful in leading your small group.

Like you, everyone who takes part in your group is entering a new system. Someone who has always played a peacemaker role, shying away from conflict and working to maintain the peace in their family of origin or among friends, is likely to take on that same role in a small group. Those who have had painful family of origin dynamics or notably negative experiences in groups often enter any new system with a level of skepticism and mistrust. Even if the leaders and other participants in a small group have good intentions, some members of the group may still respond in guarded and skeptical ways because of past experiences in relationships.

Many people bring a healthy level of guardedness to groups that should not be read as dysfunction. People choose varying levels of self-disclosure based on personal preference and comfort levels with emotionally intimate relationships. But be aware of high levels of mistrust or skepticism that you may need to treat with care and explore together to help the whole group feel emotionally secure and at ease. As a leader, try not to be highly reactive to what you notice, but take note of each member's degree of guardedness and openness in their willingness to let others get to know them.

Every group dynamic differs. Groups have people in them, which makes them complex, frustrating, fascinating, and exhausting at times. Yet groups are also deeply rich, rewarding, and full of love and opportunities for emotional and spiritual transformation. We can best experience the beauty and complexity of the body of Christ in healthy groups.

Leader Checklist for Entering the System

✓ Groups are interdependent systems, living and active.

✓ Each group member plays an important role in the system.

✓ Pay attention to what you already know through your experiences in groups, including your family of origin, friend groups, committees, or teams.

✓ People vary in their degree of openness and sharing in a group, and that is OK.

Navigate the Stages

Be patient, then, brothers and sisters, until the Lord's coming. See how the farmer waits for the land to yield its valuable crop, patiently waiting for the autumn and spring rains.
—JAMES 5:7, NIV

A therapy group typically progresses through five stages: forming, storming, norming, performing, and adjourning.[1] Small groups often go through the same progression. The table on the next page briefly describes each stage so you can refer to it as your group moves through the stages. The specific goals for small-group leaders are based on my twenty years of experience leading groups.

Understanding the progression of group stages can help you set realistic expectations and conduct an ongoing check-in with yourself about how the group is doing. There is no set time period for a stage; each group is unique in its developmental process, and these stages describe general and common patterns.

Forming

In the *forming stage*, start strong. Even if you lack confidence, you can use these basic strategies to begin effectively and project and build confidence. Try to create a comfortable environment

Group Stage	Description	Goals for Small Group Leaders
Forming	Positive, polite Anxious, excited Roles and responsibilities may be unclear	Create comfortable environment Set clear expectations Follow a predictable routine Consider written group goals or values
Storming	Conflicts may arise in communication styles Frustration may be present People evaluate facilitator's approach Authority may be challenged	Address conflict openly and directly Encourage discussion and validate multiple viewpoints Go to scripture as source of wisdom Maintain authenticity
Norming	Differences resolved Leader appreciated Closer bonds, socializing People give and receive feedback	Continue providing opportunities for discussion, feedback, and shared leadership
Performing	Group goals are achieved Tasks can be delegated Members grow and develop Feels easier to be part of the group Strong core to the group	Provide positive reinforcement and encouragement to group Look for potential leaders of future groups
Adjourning	Group ends due to restructuring or a fixed time period ending Those who value routine or have formed close bonds may find it difficult	Normalize the life stage of a group—it's OK to end Review the successes and validate each person's contribution End with a social event—lunch or dinner or activity together

based on what you know about your group's demographics and preferences. Offering coffee, tea, snacks, and/or wine can help make group members more comfortable. After all, Jesus shared wine and food with his disciples.

As group members arrive at your meeting place, you'll likely have the opportunity for small talk. As a psychologist who enjoys going straight to highly personal information and topics of deep importance, I have to remind myself that small talk is a normal social step into others' lives. As your group gathers, especially for the first time, practice non-intrusive interest. Ask group members what they like to do in their free time and who is most important to them. Ask about their interests in books, movies, or music. Basic questions and observations provide stepping-stones into deeper relationships.

Remember that group members will bring their own emotional experiences to a new group setting. Some may be uncertain of whether this group will be worth their time and energy. People may feel anxious or worry they are inadequately equipped. They may fear feeling trapped, judged, overcommitted, anxious, envious, or uncomfortable. Try to be mindful of others' discomfort. You can build empathy for this kind of discomfort by making time to attend an unfamiliar group event before your first small-group meeting. Attend a support group if you've never been to one, or visit a place of worship of another denomination or faith. The less familiar it is to you, the better.

I recently visited a friend's yoga studio and, due to Atlanta traffic and my overscheduling tendencies, I arrived late to the class. I bounded down the stairs into a dark, silent room where at least fifty people were meditating quietly. I felt a wave of embarrassment and incompetence, like an outsider who had landed in a place I didn't belong. Realizing it would be even more embarrassing to turn around and leave, I tiptoed to a place in the back of the room and quietly joined the group. Despite my rushed tardiness, the other class members smiled at me and extended a gracious welcome. We all find more capacity for empathy when we ourselves have been willing to sit with our own discomfort. We can be patient and extend warmth when people are late, unprepared, or hesitant to engage.

Be sure to keep the initial meeting within a clearly stated time frame and set expectations with clearly communicated goals and tasks. At the same time, you will want to be sure to touch on something of depth so that the group is worth everyone's time, including yours. A great way to facilitate depth is to begin the first meeting with a relaxed activity in an effort to get to know something about each person in the group. Common icebreaker games like sharing favorite colors or embarrassing moments and "forced fun" games that require movement often have the opposite effect. Instead, try to begin with an activity that lets each person engage authentically without being required to share too much personal information too quickly. A great option for small groups is to ask everyone to be prepared to share something about their spiritual journey for up to five minutes. Each person can choose whether to give a short version of their whole faith journey or describe a current devotional or prayer practice.

Size

Jesus chose to invite twelve disciples into his small group, and in my experience about eight to twelve is an excellent size. A larger group begins to feel more like a class. A smaller group may not offer enough variety in perspectives to create lively discussion and encourage spiritual growth. Group therapists suggest seven to eight as an ideal size, which can allow for more individual sharing.[2] In some scenarios the number in the group may depend upon how many are interested in joining. I think a minimum of six is a good starting point, and it is okay to build the group over time. Even adding one person at any point will change the dynamic of the group, so it is wise to decide at the beginning whether adding members is a possibility.

Setting

Establish a comfortable, welcoming setting for your group. I have often chosen to host small-group meetings in my home. Inevitably there is a mad rush to set the coffee maker, start the dishwasher, and shove random items in closets and drawers fifteen minutes before guests arrive. However, I do not have to deal with traffic or babysitters when I host at home. After leading many groups, my husband and I have learned hosting strategies that work well and those that do not. One strategy that did not work was thinking that twelve children aged three to eleven with Nerf guns could get along well in our basement while their parents engaged in focused discussion about faith. Instead, Nerf gun pellets flew as children ran in and out of the room and distracted parents took turns intervening. Dodging Nerf pellets seldom facilitates a focused spiritual mindset. We needed another plan involving a babysitter. Eventually, the timing felt off for this group, and we ended it prematurely. We needed a better plan. We have had successes hosting groups in our home after children have gone to bed or when they could be occupied by a movie for our ninety-minute meetings.

If you prefer a place other than your home, consider a coffee shop, church classroom, park, restaurant, office conference room, or a rotation of group member's homes. Plan ahead and reserve space when needed. Find out what works and adjust as needed, but keep in mind that each setting should invite and encourage focused sharing.

Structure

As a leader, you also need to choose a structure for the group and communicate the general structure to the group. In therapy groups, there are often some criteria for members, and the process often begins with a screening interview to see whether a particular client is likely to be a good fit for the group based on presenting concerns, personality dynamics, and client preferences. If your church is beginning several groups at once, similar screening questions may help place people into groups that will be a good fit for all participants. You can use these basic questions as a starting point for creating groups:

1. What is your availability (evenings, weekends, or weekdays)?
2. What type of group are you interested in attending (couples, gender-specific, or particular life stage)?
3. What type of studies are you interested in doing (books of the Bible or reading a book together)?

Maybe you've decided based on responses that certain groups are going to consist of all men, all women, all single adults, or all couples or parents. Maybe you'll decide that the group is for a particular stage of life: parents of preschoolers, older adults, parents of teens, single professionals, caregivers, or people in some sort of transitional stage. I have found that similarities in life stages but diversity in perspectives make for the most interesting and relevant discussions in groups, but there is certainly potential for a quality group experience with all types of group composition. For instance, I participated in a mixed-gender process therapy group for a couple of years around the time my first son was born. The group had the general goal of sharing feelings and providing support for one another. Some in the group were up to forty years older than me, with a wide range of life experiences and circumstances. Commonly discussed issues included family relationships, marital conflicts, parenting, personal insecurities, and self-doubt. Everyone was there for a different reason, but we had a common need for companionship, self-reflection, and understanding of ourselves and our relationships. I brought my struggles with perfectionism and decision-making to the therapy group and learned a great deal from the varying perspectives.

Small-group members bring similar concerns and needs to the group and often raise these during discussion or in prayer requests. We all have some basic needs in common: love and belonging. The therapists in my process group provided a type of parental guidance that was respectful and empowering, and the group offered a confidential, time-limited setting. I reflect on that therapy group when I think of helpful and healthy groups. Though I will likely never see the people from that therapy group again, their imprint on my life is lasting. Hearing someone my mother's age sharing her feelings toward her adult children and someone my father's age sharing his feelings about his emotional needs left powerful, lasting impressions on my life. I still remember the healing words from members of the group. It was not their job to lift me up and make me feel better, but their ability to offer healing words allows me to offer similar words of hope and affirmation to others in my life today.

Once the structure is set for the members of the group, consider the structure you'll set for the group time. The following is one example based on a flow that has worked well in groups I have led:

7:00-7:30 p.m.	Group members arrive and catch up informally over snacks and coffee
7:30-7:35 p.m.	Move from kitchen to living room and open in prayer
7:35-8:35 p.m.	Discuss the scripture and chapter(s) for the week; ask questions from a study guide if you're using one
8:35-8:55 p.m.	Group members share prayer requests
8:55-9:00 p.m.	Closing prayer

There are many possibilities for structuring the group, so experiment with a plan and find what works for your group to feel comfortable, enjoy the time together, and walk away spiritually encouraged in some way. As quickly as you can, establish a set routine that will be somewhat predictable for people from week to week.

Storming

The second group stage is the *storming stage*. Frustration may arise between group members, differences in communication styles may lead to conflict, and group members may begin to critique your leadership or challenge your authority to lead. You'll need to navigate some inevitable conflict with a spirit of clarity, kindness, and authenticity. Unspoken conflict tends to do the most damage, either by leaving everyone guessing or by allowing negative feelings to build to an outburst. If you're one who tends to avoid conflict, remember that you can address conflict with an observational statement before tension rises or an angry outburst occurs. If a group member has missed several meetings in a row without letting you know why, you can mention it in a one-on-one conversation as calmly and non-judgmentally as possible: "Hey, I just wanted to check in with you about how you're feeling in the group. You've missed a couple of meetings recently. Is there anything you want to talk about?" This type of statement opens the door to conversation and keeps you and the group from trying to guess how individual group members are feeling. Bringing the behavior into an open discussion builds trust and communicates that you have noticed and care.

Conflict is not bad; in fact, you should be concerned if *no* conflict is present. A phenomenon called groupthink can occur when group members' naturally varying perspectives become too similar to one another.[3] Pressure to conform to one opinion crowds out critical thinking and the ability to think through alternative viewpoints. Groupthink can go so far as to create dehumanizing attitudes toward those outside the group. Welcome conflict and realize that it is a natural and healthy part of group formation. As a leader, you do not need to feel threatened by perspectives that differ from your own; you can learn a lot by listening and learning from members of the group who differ from you.

Norming

In the *norming* stage, group members have a well-established bond, and the group has a strong core. The group is accomplishing its goals and moving with a more natural flow. The group has moved beyond the initial stages of basic trust and sharing, has worked through some conflict, and has established norms and goals for the group. Prayer requests may become more personal and vulnerable, and group members give and receive feedback. The group will be able to provide space for Jesus' love to move and heal as a member navigates an unforeseen struggle with a troubling mammogram, a deep regret, or anger with an estranged family member.

The love of Jesus flowing among us can provide spiritual comfort. When we cannot find the right words, we can rest in the Spirit's comfort together. We are not alone. While the Spirit cannot physically hold our hand, embrace us, or speak audible words to our pain, another person can. People—as complex and risky as they can be—are God's hands and feet, hugs and words, silent but comforting embraces. People bring us into a deeper awareness of what the love God offers can look like in everyday touch, sight, and language. People embody God's love for us in ways that we need, and it is OK to need God's love in human ways.

I have a friend whose hugs are deeply healing. When Camber hugs me, I feel like whatever is going on is going to be fine. She offers hugs freely every time I see her. Her friendship has been healing in many ways; but if hugs were all I ever received from her, she still would have made a notable influence on my experience of receiving love. Human touch and affection provide ways to experience closeness and healing, but we can also connect with one another in non-physical ways: a gentle response, kind words, an uplifting note, time set aside to listen deeply, or an unexpected gift. The common, predictable meeting place and time of a small group where we gather in the same room sharing a snack and cup of coffee can strengthen group members' relationships. Smiles, eye contact, and undistracted listening provide warmth and connection when offered in a loving way.

Performing

During the *performing* stage, the group's well-established core members may naturally begin to take on more shared leadership. In this stage, you can encourage group members in their leadership abilities and look for potential leaders of future groups.

In a meeting toward the end of a yearlong *Disciple Bible Study* through my church, we gave feedback to one another about the spiritual gifts and strengths we had seen in one another throughout the year. It is one of my most memorable small-group experiences. One woman told me she felt I was called to be an apostle or a pastor. I could not hold back tears as I absorbed the way she and others in the group looked into my eyes and shared the gifts that they saw in me. Their feedback shaped the steps I would take in the months and years that followed as I pursued a path of ministry, continued studying the Bible, and became an author.

Adjourning

Finally, the *adjourning stage* involves the challenge of ending the group well. You can end a group well when you are intentional, thoughtful, and allow space for feelings of grief and loss. An adjourning stage offers opportunities to sort out any unfinished business and share hopes for the future of relationships between group members. Some specific methods for ending well will be discussed more at length in strategy 8.

Leader Checklist for Navigating the Stages

- ✓ Consider the stage of your group in order to set realistic expectations and conduct an ongoing check-in with yourself about how the group is doing.
- ✓ In the forming stage, consider size, setting, and structure.
- ✓ In the storming stage, navigate conflict openly, directly, and with respect.
- ✓ In the norming stage, enjoy closer bonds and make space for feedback.
- ✓ In the performing stage, delegate and consider which goals have been achieved.
- ✓ In the adjourning stage, take care to communicate well and provide opportunities for group members to explore any unfinished business.

Seek Transformation

Be transformed by the renewing of your minds.

—ROMANS 12:2

One of the most valuable lessons I learned and continue to see evidenced in my personal therapy is that we are wounded in relationships, but relationships also help to heal us.[1] Personal therapy often involves reflecting on emotional wounds inflicted through negative encounters in our lives. We can all point to relational wounds, but have we all experienced relational healing? Psychology offers us the gift of understanding and experiencing corrective emotional experiences. A small-group setting can create a similar potential for the type of corrective emotional experiences that therapy groups work toward. In healthy groups, those who have experienced chaos and unpredictability in families of origin may instead begin to experience consistency and predictability; those who have experienced judgment or rigidity may find grace and flexibility.

One of my supervisors during my post-doctoral graduate training said that therapy is ultimately about helping people either loosen or tighten themselves emotionally.[2] If you find that people in your group are frequently self-critical, rule-oriented, or rigid, try to extend and model grace and flexibility while respecting their needs and comfort zone and providing structure and predictability. They may need to loosen up, but they need to do so at their own pace. Others may be a bit emotionally loose and will need you to model setting boundaries like ending prayer requests when you say you will, even though they may feel disappointed. Give them time, be patient, and know that you don't have to expand your boundaries and wear yourself out for them to benefit from the group.

Consider an adult who was not given enough permission to act capably and independently in her family of origin. In a relationship where she is encouraged to actively participate in decision-making, where her partner trusts and values her, she has an enhanced sense of personal power and can take more ownership in the relationship and in decisions related to the relationship. This relationship could be in a dating relationship, in a workplace environment, with a friend, or on a committee at church. Rather than reverting to a familiar but disempowering, harmful relational dynamic, she experiences healing.

Here's another example: A young woman shares with a new friend her experience of being harshly criticized by a former partner. The new friend creates space for the young woman's story, listens with a non-anxious presence, and extends a compassionate response. Maybe the new friend offers a hug or a willingness and availability to talk as needed over the course of time. The young woman learns that her story can be spoken, heard, and valued. She learns that people can be loving, not just critical. She learns that relationships can be healing, not just wounding. When it comes to relationships, the power of healing can transcend the power of wounding.

The capacity for emotional transformation is even more pronounced in a group setting. Group dynamics are powerful, as group members respond at once to several people. Every person brings a unique history of struggles and strengths to the group. Inevitably, we all respond to one another's dynamics and become a living system that transcends the sum of its parts. As the apostle Paul describes in 1 Corinthians 12, the body of Christ is made up of many parts. An eye or ear cannot function independently, and neither can we. When the whole body—the whole system—moves interdependently and cohesively, it can offer each part something more.

What might a corrective *spiritual* experience look like? Consider this example: A young man grew up in a church that operated with rigidity and criticism. His pastor judged his mother for getting divorced, and some church members alienated his family. Now an adult, the young man comes to a small group feeling skeptical of church people, skeptical of God, and expecting that he will need to be perfect to avoid judgment. Through relationships in the group, he begins to experience an unfamiliar grace and love that flows from a spirituality that welcomes rather than excludes, embraces rather than judges. He begins to understand God as approachable, loving, and willing to embrace him regardless of his worst moments and most misguided choices. In many church settings, we call this type of corrective experience *transformational.*

Through the group, various members show this young man the face of God. The spiritual and emotional cannot be neatly compartmentalized. Maybe his experiences with caregivers also played into his perspective toward God. Maybe his earlier choice in churches gravitated toward a familiar though unhealthy pattern of harsh judgment. Sometimes we gravitate toward unhealthy patterns just because they are familiar. Maybe for this man, entering into a grace-filled congregation was uncomfortable and different.

Just by getting together as a group, we provide an opportunity for people to cope actively with life instead of withdrawing into an isolating avoidant coping style. Most mental health problems intensify in the face of social isolation, so the social nature of the small-group experience can be both spiritually and emotionally transformative. When we avoid relationships, we can only imagine and guess at what people in our lives think and feel. To know relational truths, we have to go beyond imagining and guessing. We need to interact with people. Groups give us the opportunity to check out our assumptions and to hear that we are not perceived as negatively as we sometimes feel. We are not as undesirable as our inner critics would determine. Groups also help us keep our ego in check as we engage with others' concerns and needs. Groups that offer corrective emotional and spiritual experiences are transformational.

Leader Checklist for Seeking Transformation

- ✓ Recognize that your group offers great potential for corrective or transformational emotional and spiritual experiences.
- ✓ Model grace and flexibility while providing structure and predictability.
- ✓ Gathering as a group helps members cope actively with life rather than retreat in isolation.

Become a
Transformational Group

Let your steadfast love, O Lord, be upon us, even as we hope in you.

—PSALM 33:22

When stepping into a new role as leader, it may help you to have some guiding principles. Understanding the eleven common group therapy principles that lead to relational healing and positive change can help you check in on the health of your small group.[1] Because small groups are not therapy groups, you do not need to achieve all of these principles for your group to be transformational. Rather, you can look for these signs of a transformational group to help you gauge your group's sense of purpose.

Transformational groups instill a sense of **hope** as group members call attention to others' worthwhile perspectives and notice one another's spiritual growth. We can be sources of hope for one another: The one who drinks a bit too much witnesses the person who maintains sobriety. The one launching a child off to college observes an empty-nester embracing new passions. The one whose child repeats a grade in school learns the story of another child who repeated a grade excelling in a new peer group. The one in a crisis of faith witnesses the prayers and hard questions of another who doubts as they both show up to work out their salvation. (See Philippians 2:12.)

Transformational groups offer a sense of **universality**. As more of our communication moves to text, email, and social media and we become more physically isolated, the touch of a hand or warm energy we feel from others in face-to-face human interaction becomes more valuable. When we feel shame about our personal struggles, we further isolate. Yet we tend to carry similar types of unspoken burdens. After many years of providing group therapy, psychotherapist Irvin Yalom noted the three most common types of secrets people carry with them: a sense of being an imposter and feeling inadequate, a deep sense of alienation from others, or a secret that is sexual in nature.[2] We all need space in our lives to know we are not alone in the types of struggles we face. You may be facing one or more of these challenges, and so may every member of your group.

Transformational groups also offer **information**. The Bible offers examples of people of faith living through the human struggles of fear, doubt, grief, and other obstacles. These stories teach that such obstacles can lead to faith that is deeper and stronger for having been tested and questioned. The Bible can help people navigate faith and struggles, and many Christians learn how to use the Bible in this way in a small group. Many groups also read books that teach new spiritual skills or learn specific prayer practices together. For example, learning a prayer practice like *lectio divina* may be a one- or multi-week endeavor for a small group.[3] The book or part of the Bible you study will provide the information, and your role as leader is to facilitate discussion around the information. In a small group, you do not need to take on an advice-giving role. You can focus on participating fully in the group's learning and discussions that help all group members grow.

Transformational groups also invite members to experience **altruism**. Group members have needs that are met through providing help. You can entrust group members with various responsibilities such as providing a snack, reading scripture, or leading the group while the leader is out or through mutual confession and prayer. The group can experience altruism by serving in the community or offering support to a neighbor. One group I led came together to furnish an apartment and provide English tutoring for a refugee family. Groups offer many opportunities to come together and bear one another's burdens. (See Galatians 6:2.)

Great groups provide the opportunity to experience **a healing replay** of one's family-of-origin dynamics. As group members gravitate toward roles similar to those they played in their families of origin, the group may be able to offer the opportunity for individuals to relive old family conflicts in helpful, healing ways. For instance, if you know group members are projecting a parental dynamic onto you, you may have the opportunity to respond more lovingly than their parents typically responded. Group members who develop sibling-like relationships may have the opportunity to have less competitive, less judgmental, and more loving encounters with one another than they had with their respective siblings.

Great groups also help members develop **socializing** techniques. Emotional intelligence requires the ability to identify emotion and to communicate it in non-destructive ways. In your group, one person might model how to express anger in feeling statements with clear behavioral requests. Another person might provide an example of an expert balance between self-care and compassion for friends. Someone else can share how she tunes out distractions to listen with undivided attention. A member who reads social cues well addresses the group with clear, direct statements. Groups offer the opportunity for members to learn social skills from others and to practice them as they interact with one another.

Likewise, transformational groups allow us to practice **imitating positive behavior**. The group provides a chance to try on some new behaviors that you see modeled in others. One parent might try to adopt a nighttime prayer with her children that another parent in the group described. A young woman learns strategies for managing her stress and loneliness when her partner works late from a young man whose partner often works late. When the group leader shares questions of faith, others in the group feel permission to do the same.

Groups also encourage **interpersonal learning**. Relationships offer us the opportunity to refute our worst beliefs about ourselves by seeing ourselves in a positive light through the eyes of other people. This is the corrective emotional experience that is central to why individual and group therapy works. For years, I believed that my needs were excessive and off-putting. When I recently went through a difficult time and asked my friend Jaime whether I was being too needy, she actually laughed out loud. "You could stand to express a little more need," she said as she nearly choked on her wine. My therapist had almost the exact same reaction. Their feedback provided a corrective emotional experience for me. When I turned in my first book, I was terrified that I had somehow shared too much, had been arrogant to write a book about God, or was in over my head writing about the Bible since I did not hold a seminary degree. Trusted relationships have since taught me that anyone can speak about an experience with God and that the vulnerable stories I shared in *Revealed* were not too much for my clients, colleagues, friends, or editor. I could not have these insights on my own, through reading about vulnerability, or even through therapy. Small groups can offer the type of validation and love that interpersonal relationships offer.

Group cohesiveness is the group equivalent of the therapist-client relational bond in individual therapy. It's much more complex, however, as a group of eight to ten people bring their own lenses and experiences into the interactions of the group. The way a group flows and works together is a core determinant of whether a group will be effective.

Transformational groups make space for emotional **catharsis**, when a group member might need to cry or vent. Emotional catharsis need not be the goal or focus of the group, but group members should feel that emotional expression is welcomed, normalized, and supported. An effective leader makes space for emotion and provides statements of support rather than trying to fix the problem or make the emotion go away.

Groups benefit from exploring questions of **meaning and purpose**. Small groups often approach existential questions: What is the meaning of life? What happens after death? How do we deal with death with integrity? What is my purpose right now? As a leader, you can make space for each member to ask and work through these questions without expecting that anyone can answer them.

In a therapy group, these factors indicate that group members will be able to work toward symptom relief and personality change. Small groups work to relieve behaviors and relationships that counter spiritual development and seek to help group members live into the image of God within each person. Cultivating some or all of these principles will help your group be transformational.

Leader Checklist for Becoming a Transformational Group

Ask yourself these questions on an ongoing basis to assess the health of your group:

- ✓ Does the group offer hope?
- ✓ Does the group offer a sense of unity through a common, shared experience?
- ✓ Does the group offer helpful information?
- ✓ Does the group provide altruistic opportunities?
- ✓ Does the group provide corrective experiences?
- ✓ Does the group help with socializing?
- ✓ Do group members practice positive behaviors they see in one another?
- ✓ Does the group offer interpersonal learning?
- ✓ Is the group cohesive?
- ✓ Is there an opportunity for group members to express emotion?
- ✓ Does the group address issues of meaning and purpose?

Talk About the Process

Jesus asked, "Who touched me? . . . I noticed that power had gone out from me."

—Luke 8:45-46

Jesus set a precedent for small groups as he reclined around a table drinking wine, eating bread, and offering existential perspectives with twelve friends. I imagine him leaning on the disciple next to him while the friend rests his head on Jesus' shoulder. The disciples, buzzed and laughing, are bantering about who gets to sit by Jesus in heaven. Perhaps they become awkwardly silent and a bit guarded as Jesus says that one of them will soon turn his back on the group and another will deny knowing him. (See Luke 22:14-34.) Psychologists refer to these as process comments, statements that openly address the nature of the relationships between people in the present experience occurring among group members.

All four Gospels contain examples of Jesus making process comments during powerful interactions with his followers. When a woman who has suffered from hemorrhaging for twelve years touches the hem of Jesus' robe, Jesus asks, "Who touched me?" (Luke 8:45). The disciples note the crowds pressing in on him from all sides, and Jesus asserts that he has noticed that power has gone out from him. Together they process what is going on in the moment.

When Jesus has just finished pleading with God to remove the burden of the crucifixion, he returns to find his disciples sleeping: "Simon, are you asleep? Could you not keep awake one hour?" (Mark 14:37). Jesus directly addresses the sleepy disciples' lack of attentive prayer during a critical hour. The third time they fall asleep, Jesus says, "Are you still sleeping and taking your rest? Enough! The hour has come; the Son of Man is betrayed into the hands of sinners" (Mark 14:41). Jesus again makes process comments. He does not shy away from the truth of his surroundings. He seems able to find words for events as they unfold. Even on the cross, he speaks to God about the process: "Father, forgive them; for they do not know what they are doing" (Luke 23:34).

When Jesus approaches Mary after his resurrection, he notices her tears: "Woman, why are you weeping? Whom are you looking for?" (John 20:15). After Peter, James, and John witness the transfiguration, Jesus touches them and addresses their fear, saying, "Get up and do not be afraid" (Matt. 17:7). Jesus has more to process after Mary and Mary Magdalene witness his empty tomb. In joy and fear, Mary and Mary Magdalene run to tell the disciples. Jesus meets and greets them, saying, "Do not be afraid. Go and tell my brothers to go to Galilee; there they will see me" (Matt. 28:10). He acknowledges their fear and gives them guidance according to the events of the moment.

Many of our daily conversations are content-focused rather than process-focused. Telling stories about the past is *content*. Speaking about our current feelings or ongoing events is *process*. We easily recite the content of our lives—the past week's activities, our child's latest success, upcoming spring break or holiday plans. As we move deeper into relationships, we may move to the process-oriented discussions of defining the relationship. What does our relationship with one another mean? How are we doing spiritually and emotionally? What is bringing tears to our eyes in this moment? We make decisions to talk about it, confront it, and deal with it together. When conflict arises, we deal with it through process comments.

Transformational small groups go beyond content and move to process levels of relationship. A person can share their fear of how they are viewed by others, and another person can say, "I don't see you that way." Another can share admiration for a group member's leadership or the impact of someone's vulnerability. Someone who has an ongoing conflict with a mother or sister may find particular comfort in female connections in the group. One who feels judged by a father or brother may feel a healing grace from male members of the group. These conversations offer healing relationships.

Pay attention to your emotional experience. When you sense something is off, it probably is. If a particular topic seems to bring up strong emotion for someone in the group, comment on what you notice: "It seems like you had a strong reaction to this chapter or topic. Do you want to say anything about it?" This process comment may draw the person's attention to their in-the-moment experience. Process comments offer a gentle prompt and opening to conversations that can facilitate a deeper connection among group members. Be aware that pushing others to share can have the opposite effect and wound rather than heal. Respect whether the person is ready and willing to say more. Group members should always feel that it is their choice whether to publicly enter a vulnerable state. People know when they are ready, but they may need a gentle invitation.

Make every effort to understand and get to know what each group member brings to the group. Each person carries an invisible suitcase of prior experiences and assumptions about the future into the group with them. You can ask questions to help discern group members' assumptions, needs, and expectations. When you are able to discern where each individual is coming from, you can better understand the strengths each person brings to the group's overall dynamic and the ways you can extend empathy to group members in the face of their unique vulnerabilities and struggles. Jesus asked questions to encourage self-reflection in his listeners: "If I have told you about earthly things and you do not believe, how can you believe if I tell you about heavenly things?" (John 3:12). "Can any of you by worrying add a single hour to your span of life?" (Matt. 6:27). "Do you believe that I am able to do this?" (Matt. 9:28). "But who do you say that I am?" (Mark 8:29).

Great leaders notice and acknowledge the strengths in other people and empower them to build upon those strengths. As you get to know the people in your group, try to focus on the benefits that each person brings to others' lives. When group members can identify and describe emotions in the moment, you will see the group come alive.

Leader Checklist for Talking About the Process

- ✓ Note the difference between content and process comments.
- ✓ Make process comments about emotions and reactions you notice to draw group members into deeper relationships.

Start Strong in the First Meeting

Those who wait for the LORD shall renew their strength, they shall mount up with wings like eagles, they shall run and not be weary, they shall walk and not faint.

—ISAIAH 40:31

Your first meeting will go a long way in setting the tone for the life of the group. Some preparation and communication with your group beforehand will help your group start strong in the first meeting. As I mentioned in the introduction, you'll want to start with an activity that helps group members get to know one another in a meaningful way. Before your first meeting, email all group members to let them know what to expect. You can provide them with logistical details, your expectations for their consistent attendance, and the prompt for your introductory activity so that everyone can prepare as they wish.

An example introductory email to the group may look something like this:

Hello and welcome to our small group!

I am glad you'll be in our group this year. We will meet weekly on Tuesday evenings from 7:00–9:00 p.m. We'll spend the first thirty minutes informally socializing. We will begin our formal group meeting with prayer at 7:30. On our first night, I'd like each person to share some of their faith journey. You can share as much or as little as you like in about five minutes. Shorter than that is fine. Here are some questions that' may serve as helpful prompts as you think about what to share with the group:

1. *If you were raised in a church or faith community, what was it like?*
2. *What was it like to convert to Christianity, go through a period of separation from Christianity, or have a significant transformation in your beliefs?*
3. *What have you liked or not liked about your previous experiences in small groups?*
4. *What are you hoping to gain from this study? What particular topics do you want to study or discussions do you hope to have with this group?*

I am glad you've decided to join this study, and I look forward to seeing you on Tuesday!

Angela

Faith backgrounds vary greatly. An experience of infant baptism and confirmation in a mainline denomination looks different from a baptism immersion ceremony in a megachurch projected on a jumbotron for thousands to witness. (I've done both just to make sure I was covered.) Share something about your own cultural background and invite group members into an open discussion of cultural differences. For some participants, five minutes of telling their faith story will feel like an eternity; for others it will sound like far too short a time frame.

If you choose to share your faith journey first, you can set the tone for the degree of self-disclosure you feel is appropriate. Model vulnerability but keep some healthy boundaries. You do not need to share an undisclosed family secret for the first time, but go beyond a surface-level introduction. Share about a tough relationship or tell the story of a major turning point in your life. You might reference a time in your life when you questioned God or wrestled with questions of faith. Sharing your faith struggles can grant others permission to share their own doubts. If you clean up your story too much, others may view you as excessively guarded or as someone who cannot relate to their faith struggles. The following is a bullet-point version of what I might share with a new group:

- I was baptized, raised, and confirmed in the Lutheran Church, but I attended many different types of churches during my college and young adult years.

- During high school and college, I went through a period of serious doubt and questioning and have been on a journey ever since to figure out what I believe. Counseling helped me overcome personal struggles (with a group of people I do not know, I will be vague about my struggles; with a group where most of us already know one another, I might specify that my struggles included an eating disorder), and my experience with counseling led me to become a psychologist.

- I've struggled with feelings of self-doubt and self-criticism but have learned to talk myself through it and consistently find support in close relationships with friends and my husband, Dusty.

- At this point in my journey I'm learning to sit with difficult questions and maintain faith amid uncertainty and seeking to understand the role I can and want to have within the church.

Over time, I've gotten comfortable sharing more personal layers of my story. In deciding how much you are willing to share, strive for balance. Reflect on your experience after sharing a story. If you didn't feel quite satisfied with the depth of your sharing and have begun to trust your group, push yourself beyond your comfort zone to be more vulnerable next time. If you feel highly anxious about what you shared, you may need to guard your heart a little more lovingly. It may be wise to hold back and share in bits and pieces over time as you build a greater sense of trust with members of your group.

Note how much group members choose to share and what the major dynamics of their lives have been. Have they experienced the safety and security of a supportive faith community? Did they have parents and caregivers who actively nurtured faith and openly discussed it? Do they mention times of alienation or frustration with their church or faith communities? Do they mention highly personal struggles, and does their disclosure seem to fit with the degree of closeness built in the relationships within the group? You'll learn a wealth of information about each person as well as information about their backgrounds that might play into future group dynamics. You might want to begin a prayer journal just for your prayers for the group. After each person tells their five-minute faith journey or after the meeting, write brief notes about significant elements of each person's story so that you can pray for the needs and experiences of the group. These spiritual journey stories may reveal wounds in each person's life that God may guide your group to help heal. The connections that begin with sharing your faith journey in the first meeting lay the groundwork for your group to be transformational.

New relationships can be intimidating. We have to negotiate together a balance of giving and receiving. Each leader and group member needs to become comfortable with both ends of that equation. We have to keep showing up for one another and be willing to work out that balance. In the early stages of a relationship, we work to understand that balance and choose what we will ask of others and what we can give to others. It's a time of asking relational questions, and communication is essential:

- May I email you between meetings if I have a question about something in the reading?
- Should I still come to the group if I have not done the reading for the week?
- Would you like to meet outside of the group time for coffee?

We test the waters and find out the level of willingness in another person to participate in closeness. Pain and conflict can result when one person desires a different level of closeness than another, but honest exchanges are vital in order to be in relationships with integrity and know where we stand with one another. Discrepancies in people's desire for closeness with one another are bound to happen, but the imbalance is best negotiated openly and with respect for one another: "I can't commit to weekly lunches, but I would enjoy getting together. How about meeting for coffee monthly?" or "I hope we can spend time connecting and catching up during group time. At this point, I can't make space for meetings outside of group time."

It is important for you to set clear boundaries and expectations. Your clarity and confidence about the group will translate into a positive start to the experience for group members.

Leader Checklist for Starting Strong in the First Meeting

✓ Before the first meeting, clearly communicate what group members can expect as you gather.

✓ Set the tone for vulnerability and boundaries in getting to know one another through your five-minute faith journeys.

✓ Make note of what you observe about group members' personalities, willingness to share, and potential group dynamics.

✓ Set clear expectations and boundaries for yourself and empower group members to set their own.

SECTION 2

Eight Strategies for Leading Well

STRATEGY 1
Practice Faith

He has told you, O mortal, what is good; and what does the LORD require of you but to do justice, and to love kindness, and to walk humbly with your God?

—MICAH 6:8

As I wrote this book, my imperfect faith practice looked something like this: I wake to my phone's alarm and snooze it until 6:09 a.m., when I reluctantly roll out of bed and realize my fourth grader, Caleb, needs to head out the door in twenty minutes. I make his lunch while my husband, Dusty, wakes him and makes breakfast, and I replay the events of the *Big Little Lies* episodes I watched the night before, trying to figure out who died. I scoop coffee into the Keurig pod and talk myself through my fatigue by revisiting my gratitude that Caleb won the county's magnet school lottery. Dusty takes Caleb to his bus stop, and I have ten or fifteen minutes to squeeze in my faith practice before I shower, wake up Zach, and begin part two of three of our getting-the-kids-out-the-door routine. On mornings when Dusty travels, the few minutes for devotional time disappear. Fortunately, he doesn't travel often, and those fifteen minutes afford me a small window of opportunity before the day unfolds.

If I can find my prayer beads, I pick them up and assume a meditative posture on the couch next to our kitchen, close my eyes, and pray. I may also grab my *Upper Room Disciplines* devotional.[1] My bookmark reminds me how long it's been since I last read it. I try not to get discouraged and remind myself that some scripture study is better than none. I absorb the short daily reading, and on my good days I read the accompanying scripture passage. On really good days I write a response in my journal. I close my eyes again and touch the beads. Some days each bead is a dilemma weighing on my heart. Other days, the beads are people in pain for whom I'm praying. Or the beads are bursts of gratitude for recent treasured encounters I've had with loved ones—an anniversary celebration with Dusty, a conversation with a friend, a much-needed word of affirmation from someone in a recent text or phone call, an opportunity to speak to a group, a friend who comes over to help me organize my home, a friend who allows me to cry and doesn't try to fix my problem. As I touch each bead, for a moment my spirit stills and my heart embraces that person, request, or painful place within me. I take deep breaths, and the beads keep me focused on my prayer. Sometimes I sense God's presence, or a particular word, phrase, or scripture passage comes to mind and I embrace it as my focus for the day. I open my eyes and see that it's time to wake up Zach. Soon it will be time to wake up Carlson. I take one more deep breath and then go into my day a little more centered, a little more patient, a little less worried. This is my current faith practice.

As we lead Bible studies, we need to carve out time for our own faith practices. Faith is a lifelong process of learning, shaping, and reshaping our understandings. Paul urges us to "work out your own salvation, with fear and trembling" (Phil. 2:12). We can work out our salvation with tools like prayer beads, meditation, a morning walk, or some other form of prayer. If we really are working out our salvation, fear and trembling will be involved. But we'll find comfort and a transcendent peace in God. We can enter boldly into the spaces of fear and trembling, working out our salvation as we go. Even though we haven't arrived at some final destination of faith, we can still lead. In fact, it may be a great relief for members of our small groups for leaders to acknowledge that we have not yet arrived either.

Our faith practices help our faith mature. We present our hopes, fears, needs, and requests to God through prayer, and meditation helps us listen for God's response. Acts of service move us beyond professing the gospel to living it. When we attend church, a community of believers strengthens us and helps us reorient our lives around loving God and loving others. Our personal practices that lead to spiritual peace and fullness allow us to give more of ourselves to our group members.

Jesus regularly spent time in prayer and solitude before giving and ministering to others. (See Luke 6:12.) We may not rise at dawn and go for a hike in the mountains before taking on the day, but we can find five minutes for our favorite prayer practice—or at least time for five deep breaths—before preparing for or leading our group meeting. Finding even one focused minute or taking one single deep breath that allows us to listen to God follows Jesus' model. When I connect with God first, my other relationships flow from that time of prayer and centeredness in a more grounded and fulfilling way. If I receive criticism after a moment with God, I am less likely to be thrown off course and personalize it. If I encounter negativity but have had five minutes to pray with my prayer beads, I am more likely to empathize with a person who may be going through something difficult. If I spend time with a friend, I more readily go out of my way to let that friend know how much she means to me and the strengths I see in her. If I see clients, I am less likely to feel burdened by trying to facilitate change and instead to trust the process and offer hope.

The following practices may help you stay grounded in your own faith as you enter into the activities of discipleship, especially as a small-group leader. Choose at least one intentional practice during the course of the group you lead. The faith practice you choose will serve as a foundation for the remaining strategies in this book. These three practices have provided accountability and help me stay focused spiritually when I am leading a small group.

1. Follow a daily devotional. *The Upper Room Disciplines* offers depth and a variety of perspectives with devotions from different authors each week. Each day suggests a scripture passage followed by some insights and a brief prayer or reflection. You can walk away with a quick but challenging anecdote that enhances your faith. Its short length and small size mean I can carry it with me and find a few minutes later in the day if I don't have time to read it before leaving the house in the morning. Choose any devotional you like because if you don't like it, you won't read it.

2. Use prayer beads. Years ago, one of my clients introduced me Kristen E. Vincent's book *A Bead and a Prayer*.[2] The book explains the concept and practice of using Protestant prayer beads to enhance and facilitate focused prayer. The beads provide a tangible way to stay focused while I pray.

68

For me, the beads provide a constant reminder and sense of God's presence. Each bead can represent a member of your group or the prayer requests they've each brought to your attention. You can use them as you ask God for guidance in different areas of your life or in implementing the strategies in this book. Be creative in using the beads for prayer, or use the methods Vincent suggests in her book.

3. Meditate daily. There are many ways to practice Christian meditation, and J. Dana Trent offers a beginner's guide through five of them in her forty-day study *One Breath at a Time*.[3] In meditation I listen for God's voice. Often, I do some combination of prayer and meditation during my brief morning devotional time. Find a practice that you can enjoy and that allows you to connect with God.

You may begin your practice by spending five minutes each morning reading a devotional or doing another spiritual practice that centers your mind on God. Choose something engaging enough that you will do it daily, and keep any materials you need in the same place to make it as easy as possible for yourself. Keep a journal, pen, and devotional next to your bed so they are available when you wake or before you go to sleep. Record your reflections and insights about your small group. You are likely to have ideas and hopes as well as doubts and hesitations regarding the group process. Bring all of your conflicts, concerns, and celebrations to God in prayer. Make time to pray for each group member at some point weekly. You may choose to keep a list of group members' prayer requests and concerns in your journal to prompt you to pray for them. A daily or weekly routine will encourage you to spend time in prayer and reflection.

As you use any of these personal practices, consider social practices that will help your faith mature. Find a way to serve others by volunteering at your church or in the community or by pausing to listen to someone going through a difficult time. Advocating for marginalized groups in your community who need support can help you be a role model for the members of your group and keep your group from becoming too inwardly focused. The presence of faith practices is more important than the perfection of faith practices. Levels of stress, commitments, and family needs ebb and flow, and you can adjust accordingly. When you prioritize your faith practices, you build an important foundation for leading well.

Leader Checklist for Practicing Faith

✓ Define what your personal faith practice will be as you lead a group. Look at it as a foundation for the rest of the strategies in this section.

✓ Spend five minutes each morning reading a devotional or doing another spiritual practice that centers your mind on God. Choose something engaging enough that you will do it daily, and keep any materials you need in the same place to make it as easy as possible for yourself.

✓ Make time to pray for each group member. Find a few minutes on your own before and after each group meeting to pray and listen for God's wisdom. Share with God your ideas, hesitations, doubts, and hopes for the group.

✓ Carve out time for social practices like volunteering or advocating for marginalized members of the community.

STRATEGY 2

Focus

Prepare your work outside, get everything ready for you in the field; and after that build your house.

—PROVERBS 24:27

As three close friends and I prepared to go on a beach trip, we planned who would room with whom. We'd never traveled together before, but some of us had trained together in Taekwondo and we all had enjoyed drinks, dinners, and dancing together. We talked about who would be reading by the pool, playing beach volleyball, and venturing out to local sightseeing and activity destinations. We were establishing our goals—to have fun, relax, and share some time away. We discussed who would cry, who was uncomfortable with crying, and who was medicated enough to make crying unlikely. We shared stories of past trips and our hopes for the coming vacation.

In many ways, a small group can be no more complex or intimidating than a beach trip with friends: We agree on a destination, chart the course, and allow for flexibility and some variety in our preferences. We make some independent choices and collaborate on other decisions. No matter how much planning we do, we can only discover how it will play out when we set out on our journey.

Conflict is inevitable. One day on our beach trip, three of us ventured out into the Caribbean on a catamaran. Nyree and Michelle began to argue about how and where to steer the boat. They each gripped the handle with equal force while I propped up my leg on the sail and sipped my mimosa. In the face of conflict, our unfiltered personalities emerged. Having virtually no experience with boats or steering them, my role was to diffuse the conflict with humor. Through their collective sailing expertise (and no help from me or my mimosa), we safely returned to shore at the end of our allotted time frame. The catamaran trip didn't go completely as planned, but we shared plenty of laughter and a collective sense of victory that brought us closer when we returned to the beach. If we can come together around a common focus and love one another through conflicts, our relationships can thrive.

Ideally, small groups can offer some of the same amenities as a beach vacation with friends: a place to relax, snacks and drinks, meaningful conversations, emotional support, fun, and something outside of your day-to-day work and responsibilities. Everyone is investing something in the group and looking for a positive experience with meaningful connections. For the group to be successful, you'll need to collaborate on some decisions. You will need to name the goals and values that provide a focus for the group. Articulate your goals for the group over the course of your time together, and ask for input from group members to develop a common understanding about why the group is gathering and what you hope to gain or accomplish by meeting together.

An early discussion about group goals can help prevent confusion and conflict later on. Each group member may have personal goals for their experience in the group (learn more about the Bible, connect socially, develop a consistent prayer practice). But if the group's goals are too loosely defined, members may feel like no one knows why you are meeting together, and the commitment and focus in the group may fade quickly. In my practice of Taekwondo, each person has individual goals (like earning a black belt or breaking two thick boards), but everyone understands that the ultimate goal of the practice is to grow into the five foundational tenets: courtesy, integrity, perseverance, self-control, and indomitable spirit. While our practice at each class includes learning forms, gaining strength, and earning belts, these five tenets clarify our focus and drive our progression in the practice. These larger goals provide structure and predictability in balance with an art form that transcends the moment. The focus drives people to high levels of commitment to the practice.

Social work professor Brené Brown suggests a practice of choosing two values to live by and developing a way of assessing for ourselves when we are living by each value and when we are not living by them.[1] She encourages us to identify behaviors that support our values and behaviors that are outside our values. Integrity and compassion are my guiding values. This means I am motivated by integrity and compassion and assess all aspects of my life through those values. I have defined ways to know when I'm living with integrity and from a place of compassion and how to know when my integrity and compassion are compromised.

Your group may benefit from identifying two or three values that will guide and focus your work and then defining how you know when your group study and discussion are being guided by those values and how you know when you have strayed from them. Maybe your group decides that faith, hope, and love will be your underlying values. Or maybe you will embrace service, scripture, and stability. Whatever your values, be sure they are simple and clear. Take time to decide together using behavioral terms how you will know when you are living by your group's values in your meetings and how you will know when your values have been compromised.

As you establish these goals, consider how they will help your faith mature. You can hold up your group's values and goals to Jesus' life as reflected in scripture: Will your goals help you ask challenging questions, unhindered by the need for approval from some outside authority? Will they guide you to show love to the most marginalized members of your community? Will they help guide and strengthen you when your discussion or reading tests your faith? Will they help you prioritize God?

You do not need to fear choosing the wrong focus or obsessing over which values are best. If your group's guiding values aren't working well, you can find new ones. To find your group's focus words, ask each person to suggest a few words for the group. Then discuss commonly suggested words and build upon or combine ideas to develop a central focus together. Write them down and provide everyone with a copy. Revisit the values during prayer and discussion often enough that people remain mindful of them. From time to time, ask the group to assess whether your time together is reflecting these values. Your group's clearly defined goals and values will serve as a powerful reminder of your intended focus when the stakes are high or emotions run strong.

Leader Checklist for Focusing

✓ Establishing a clear focus for your group prevents conflict and confusion.

✓ Decide on two or three core values that will guide your group.

✓ Ensure that everyone in the group knows the goals/values by discussing them together, writing them down, and providing everyone with a copy.

✓ Reference and revisit the values often. From time to time, ask the group to assess whether your time together is reflecting these values.

STRATEGY 3
Stretch but Not Too Far

Bear one another's burdens, and in this way, you will fulfill the law of Christ. . . . For all must carry their own loads.
—GALATIANS 6:2, 5

Boundaries are healthy limits that we put in place to ensure emotional security. They keep us from resentment, betrayal toward ourselves and others, and self-sabotaging behaviors. Boundaries help us discern where we end and another person begins so that we do not become fused with others in unhealthy ways. As is often the case, spiritual maturity requires holding two truths at once: We can bear one another's burdens *and* carry our own load. While we are an interdependent body of believers, we each hold an individual identity like an ear or an eye, a hand or a foot. We are responsible for what falls within our boundaries: thoughts, feelings, urges, desires, and preferences. It's not in our best interest to expect others to take responsibility for those aspects of our experiences. Neither is it in our best interest to take responsibility for those areas of other adults' lives. Even as group leaders, we are not responsible for how a group member responds to a passage of scripture, whether two group members enter into conflict, or whether our group likes the book chosen for the study. Those aspects of the group process are out of our control and fall within other people's boundaries.

If you struggle with knowing where to set your limits, you might want to make a list of which aspects of the group are in your control and which are not. For example, you may be in control of the meeting time and place, the book or passages of the Bible the group will study, and the general structure and questions you present to the group during the meeting. You are in control only of how *you* respond when members of the group disagree. You do not control whether people benefit spiritually from reading that book or scripture, whether members of the group feel led by the Holy Spirit to make changes in their lives, or whether two members of the group agree on an issue within the church or interpretation of a particular passage of scripture. You can, however, choose to remain calm and make space for various perspectives and even heated, emotional discussions in a group. People can disagree. The group can continue to thrive.

In every relationship, we negotiate boundaries. We set physical boundaries by giving indications of the level of touch with which we are comfortable. We negotiate how much time we are willing to spend on others and how deep we are willing to go in conversation. We set boundaries on how much of our time, money, and possessions we share or give away. We learn and communicate how close to another person we can tolerate getting emotionally. Through conversations and nonverbal interactions, our groups will find boundaries between the leader and the group as a whole, the leader and each individual member, and between members.

It may help for you as the leader to decide where you antici-
pate setting boundaries before the group begins to meet. To do
so, ask yourself the following questions:

- How long am I okay with the group staying after our
  meetings end for some extra informal socializing?
- Is it acceptable for group members to miss a group? How
  should absences be communicated to me?
- If group members want to meet with me outside of group
  time, how much time am I able or willing to devote to
  those meetings?
- If it is not predetermined before the group begins, who
  will choose the book or book of the Bible we study?
- How will I handle disagreements in group decisions? Will
  I take a vote or make an executive decision?

Be clear and consistent about your boundaries. Some people may pull you to extend your boundaries or prompt you to
fall into a familiar role from your family of origin. I have been
managing others' high levels of anxiety since I was a young
child, so soothing another person's anxiety is well within my
comfort zone. When I meet a highly anxious client, I feel a
huge amount of empathy and want to equip them to live life in
a freer and less anxious way. Because I am comfortable in this
dynamic, I need to set adequate boundaries with highly anxious
clients. I also set boundaries with highly anxious people in my
daily life because treating everyone I meet as a client would
be unwise and emotionally taxing. The boundary between my
professional and personal life is important for me to set. I want
to help my friends, listen to them, talk through issues, and love

them well; I help connect friends with therapists, but my friendships play out differently than my relationships with clients.

Deciding how, when, and where to set boundaries can be difficult. Boundaries that are too rigid or too loose can affect your group's cohesiveness. Trust your comfort zone and your sense of what is right for you, and seek out an experienced leader who can talk through setting boundaries with you. Sometimes setting boundaries is trial-and-error process. You may discover that you've overextended yourself in providing so much emotional support to a group member that you feel depleted and begin to sacrifice your own self-care. If you feel out of balance, you are not loving self as neighbor and neighbor as self. A feeling of resentment is a sign that you need to adjust your boundaries. If you can say yes to helping someone without feeling resentment, you are within your boundaries. If you cannot, consider helping that person find others to reach out to when you are not available and draw some clear limits around when you are available. Try to examine degrees of availability rather than thinking in all-or-nothing terms. If someone wants you to spend a long time on the phone with them, try taking the call but letting them know how much time you have to devote to the call and stick to your boundary.

I encourage you to pay attention to the responses various members of the group elicit in you. Do you tend to feel warm and protective? Irritated and impatient? Parental and nurturing? Curious and affectionate? Attracted? Uncomfortable? Resentful? Who elicits which responses from you? Take a moment and write down in your journal each group member's name along with the feelings that come up for you. Be curious and nonjudgmental about the feelings you notice. Allow all your feelings to be present; no matter what you feel, you can make wise decisions about how to proceed. Notice patterns. Consider what emotions are related to your current dynamic with the group member and what may have something to do with your past experiences. Do you respond differently to men than women? Does anyone in the group remind you of a family member? These questions may help you identify the types of people that tend to push your boundaries and help you become proactive in setting firmer boundaries.

Beginning and ending the group on time, staying on topic with a balance of flexibility and structure, and making expectations clear are all ways to honor one another's boundaries. These practices honor people's time and provide some predictability so people can relax into the group and let go of the anxiety that comes with the unknown. Honor the time that your group members have set aside for the group. Some may have babysitters to get home to or other reasons to leave. When you're deep in discussion but approaching the end of the group time, try saying, "This is a great discussion, and I hope we can pick up here next time. I'm going to shift to our closing prayer, in case there's anyone who needs to leave at 9:00. If anyone wants to stay and talk more, you are welcome to stay." Or, if your boundaries limit socializing after the meeting, "Will you all join me to close in prayer? There may be other prayer requests so let's communicate via email about anything that hasn't come up yet and leave more time for prayer at the end of next week's discussion."

A good leadership boundary is to allow group members to assume some of the responsibility for the group's functioning. Try to discourage a dynamic where the group depends solely on you for energy or guidance. Too much authority in a leader can foster dependency and immature behavior in the members. Psychotherapist Irvin Yalom provides the metaphor of moviegoers.[1] Some people attend a group as though they are attending a movie, but leaders can encourage the group to *be the movie.* Interaction between members is the point of the group. Your role is not to entertain but to facilitate a life-giving, authentic interaction between members of the body of Christ who each have a unique perspective and energy to bring to the group. The members animate the group with life, plot, action, and resolution.

Sometimes the plot begins to intensify and feels hard to manage. One example of this is when group members project family of origin experiences onto God or others in the group. Our original connections with caregivers set a profound precedent for our interpersonal relationships. When needs are not met in those formative years, we tend to approach adult relationships trying to work out those experiences around our unmet needs.

Someone may have a strong reaction to you or another person in the group that is difficult to make sense of. *Transference* is a term used in psychology that refers to a person's reaction to you that actually has to do with someone else in that person's life. Maybe one of your group members is remembering what it was like to have a critical and authoritarian parent, so he responds to your gentle feedback in ways that suggest you are also critical and authoritarian. You are puzzled because you really tried to be warm and affirming. It's not your job to take on others' unmet needs or help them resolve transference, but knowing that they may appear in your group can help you empathize with their personal pain and set boundaries. You can address strong emotional reactions by using process comments to put the responsibility on the person to express their needs rather than taking on the burden of trying to guess at a solution to the problem.

As a leader, model and encourage vulnerability and openness, but rein in high levels of emotionality that can derail the group from your goals. Though they can offer similar benefits, small groups are not therapy groups. Small groups provide emotional support for group members as they grow spiritually, but part of being a leader with healthy boundaries is knowing when to refer someone for additional support. Great leaders know their limits. Do not hesitate to talk with a pastor or therapist about resources that could help your group member feel added support. Websites like www.psychologytoday.com serve as a great resource for connecting individuals with a therapist, and some churches offer free support groups or discounted therapy to church members. Talk to the person one-on-one outside the group about these resources and opportunities. If someone seeks individual therapy or group therapy, you may see that person relax into healthier boundaries and the intended goals of your small group.

Boundaries should not be so rigid that there is no room for unexpected discussions. Be patient in listening to a group member's story, even if it doesn't seem immediately relevant to what you planned to discuss. You may be able to tie it back to the topic at hand, or the person may need to share the story to be able to focus on the group discussion. Be flexible; allow your people to take precedence over staying on task. When a person in the group has had a particularly joyful celebration or intense struggle during the past week, make time to acknowledge it in the group. Don't abandon your plan altogether but allow space for your group members to share their lives with one another.

One of my most memorable small-group meetings was a few months after I had a miscarriage in 2008. I had been carrying a lot of sadness, and though group members often checked in with me, on that particular night the weight of my loss was powerful and deeply sad. The group created time and space to come around me, share tears with me, and pray with me. It gave me great comfort amid my loss, and I will never forget the group's love, flexibility, and sensitivity to my needs.

We need other people. Groups can be transformational because they give us the opportunity to find relief in sharing our pain or to hear validation that we cannot locate within ourselves. Sometimes we lack flexibility and need a push from others. When I returned to Taekwondo after a long break, I felt stiff and awkward, and my legs tired quickly. It felt impossible to lift them kick after kick after kick. From time to time in Taekwondo class, we would stretch in pairs so that we could physically push one another further than we could go alone. Progress can be uncomfortable, and we often resist it for ourselves. A partner can see our capability and push us past where we might give up on our own.

My clients with eating disorders often have adopted extremely rigid rules and practices around food. In the same way a fellow Taekwondo student pushes my leg deeper into a stretch, I push my clients to eat foods that seem risky, scary, or "off limits" to them. I cannot push too hard, but I can see where their limits can be stretched. It gets uncomfortable, but soon they learn to be more flexible on their own with food choices.

Consider the ways you may need to allow others to push you in your degree of flexibility regarding other peoples' perspectives, the structure and flow of the group, and biblical interpretation. What do others see in a particular passage of scripture or insight from the study that you may have missed? Pay attention to how you can push others in their own degree of flexibility by inviting them to share more about themselves, their faith journeys, and their perspectives on scripture. The group can become truly transformational when you invite others to explore and share experiences of doubt and uncertainty in faith. Your group members will grow in faith when you allow everyone to be stretched, and healthy boundaries will help you make sure you don't stretch too far.

Leader Checklist for Stretching but Not Too Far

- ✓ Set clear boundaries to ensure an emotionally healthy group.
- ✓ Seek wisdom from your pastor and other leaders if you're having trouble knowing what healthy boundaries look like.
- ✓ Consider what is in versus out of your control.
- ✓ Clear boundaries are not just for you; they allow the group to relax into some predictability and relieve anxiety that comes from the unknown.
- ✓ Empower group members to take an active role rather than attending as "moviegoers."
- ✓ Know your limits, and refer people to more help and support when you sense that they could benefit from it.

✓ Encourage vulnerability and openness, but rein in high levels of emotionality that derail the group from its goals.

✓ Maintain flexibility, inviting openness to learn from the members of your group. Others can push you beyond your comfort zone in helpful ways.

STRATEGY 4
Listen Well

You must understand this, my beloved: let everyone be quick to listen, slow to speak, slow to anger.

—JAMES 1:19

Effective small-group leadership requires active listening. This type of leadership is an opportunity not to lecture but to invite people into authentic engagement and to prompt meaningful discussion. Active listening skills will help you hear the current needs of the group and respond in ways that encourage vulnerable sharing and spiritual growth. Your main role may be to get others to talk and to listen acutely so that you can engage with genuine concern and love. You can develop your active listening skills by focusing on nonverbal elements that communicate your interest and attentiveness. Make eye contact and lean in toward the person speaking. Nod and offer minimal encouragers that let the speaker know that you are listening. Authenticity is key. You can practice your active listening skills with anyone. Listening well may be the most important part of your role as a group leader and can create moments of connection. You may notice that as you talk less, your group reaches a state where everyone is engaged and participating in the same moment and transformation occurs.

Make sure you are taking care of yourself well enough to come to your group meeting with energy and willingness to really listen to others. Eat enough, drink enough water, and get enough rest. Try to schedule less responsibility and workloads on the day of the week when you lead your group. Leave some margin in your schedule so that you can prepare for your group meetings a few days in advance. These strategies will help you be emotionally and spiritually present, not just physically present with your group. I do not remember many details of the topics or studies of my small groups, but I remember who actively listened to me and who authentically cared about me.

If you have many concerns in your life, try to set them aside before your group meeting begins. One strategy is to jot down your concerns in a journal and know that you will return to address them later. Setting them aside will help you more mindfully focus on your group.

A related listening skill is non-anxious listening, when we understand that our role is to listen without trying to offer solutions. We can offer our presence to people amid their complex problems, listen actively, and let go of anxiety that drives us to rid ourselves and others of pain. Our faith can help us. God offers us the truth about pain and suffering through Jesus: "In the world you face persecution. But take courage; I have conquered the world" (John 16:33). In Jesus, we cannot have freedom from trouble, but we can have peace. When those around us are suffering, we can pray for peace, for wholeness, and for God's comfort. We need not offer explanations or speak at length (or at all) about the value or joy in suffering. Our expressions of God's love can be enough.

If all your best efforts to be well rested and well prepared so that you can provide an active and non-anxious listening presence for your group have failed, just show up. I have shown up to lead when I was exhausted and sleep-deprived after the births of three children, when I was grieving the deaths of friends and family members, and when I was just distracted by my mental to-do list for the evening or my own emotional conflicts and processes. Give what you can. You can still show up to lead when you're not feeling 100 percent, but take care of yourself. It's okay to occasionally ask a group member to step up and lead while you step back or stay home. Try not to cancel group meetings because that can sacrifice the stability of the group. Even if there's low attendance on a particular week, keep holding the group meetings to communicate that you value the time and honor the people who are able to be there. I've had meaningful groups with two other people, and we walked away from it glad that I had not canceled the meeting. Extend grace and maintain a welcoming environment by encouraging group members to attend even when they have not completed the reading or can only be there for a portion of the time. Through active and non-anxious listening, you will communicate authentic care and strong leadership. Through generous self-care, you will show up ready to lead well.

Leader Checklist for Listening Well

✓ Active listening is a skill set you can practice with eye contact, attentive posture, and verbal indications.

✓ Practice generous self-care and leave some margin in your life.

✓ Prepare in advance and set aside your concerns so you can be fully present and let group members know they are heard.

✓ Let go of any anxious need to fix problems. Scripture normalizes human problems and promises peace and wholeness.

✓ If all your plans and preparations fail, you can still show up and do your best to listen actively and non-anxiously. Invite group members to do the same.

STRATEGY 5
Know and Share Yourself

First clean the inside of the cup, so that the outside also may become clean.

—MATTHEW 23:26

I strive for self-sufficiency in everything I do. Impossible as that is for anyone, I continue to convince myself that it's attainable, so I felt particularly vulnerable when I asked my friend Camber for help. Camber's house is one of the most organized places I've ever seen, so I asked her to come over to give me some input on my organizational challenges. We walked through my house and systematically opened each closet, drawer, and storage space. My messes became obvious and visible. She offered feedback about my overflowing and chaotic spaces in a creative, humorous, and non-intrusive way. I sensed she was genuinely invested. With a fresh set of eyes, she offered incredibly helpful suggestions. As we created an organization plan, she related to my current parenting challenges, listened as I processed some feelings about my relationships, and dealt kindly with my internal messes too. Spending time with my friend was different than reading a book or a blog about house organization. Her validation and the personal encouragement of our relational exchanges motivated me to change my organizational habits in ways I never would have after reading a book. I walked away with a clearer sense of how to organize and deal with my organizational and emotional messes. I had gained a page of notes and an ally.

Your ability to look inside your psychological drawers and cabinets and be honest about your strengths, limitations, and biases will help you discover hard truths about yourself and will increase your capacity for vulnerability. Knowing and sharing hard truths about yourself will facilitate an environment where all group members feel free to share their perspectives and experiences. You will be a more effective leader if you know yourself well enough to set aside your feelings and reactions to group members and adopt an approachable and non-defensive stance. If you are able to receive feedback from your group without needing excessive affirmation, you will be able to take in the true and valuable parts and let the rest go. If you are true to yourself and the group's vision, you can adapt and make changes as needed.

If you've engaged in your own personal therapy, self-reflective journaling, spiritual direction, or any process of focused reflection, you should have some self-awareness about your strengths and challenges as a leader. If you'd like to expand your self-awareness, consider a study such as *Revealed*.[1] You also may consider exploring your Enneagram type or StrengthsFinder profile.[2,3] I tend to resist being boxed into a category (which I'm told means I'm an Enneagram 4), but I can appreciate how some categorical processes can help us gain insight into our own patterns and how they differ from others'. These popular categorical tests have their limitations. Personality psychologists consistently point toward the "Big Five" personality traits, which are measured on a continuum of low to high rather than categorical types. Though less well-known to the general public, they have better research support and allow for a wider range of individual differences. You can take free inventories online and find out where you are on a continuum of extroversion, neuroticism, agreeableness, conscientiousness, and openness to experience.[4]

The human experience makes all of us good candidates for individual or group therapy. I don't know anyone who has not benefited or could not benefit from doing some therapy. Some people never will seek therapy, and that is OK because it's not the only way to heal. But there is unique potential in a solid therapeutic relationship to receive feedback that other people in your life are less likely to share with you, to build a trusting relationship unlike any other, to explore highly vulnerable feelings in a confidential way, and to create a space for healing outside of your everyday life and routines.

Knowing my strengths and challenges has served me well as a group leader. In the self-awareness I gain through individual therapy and spiritual reflection, I've learned that I am prone to wonder whether I am too much or not enough for people, and it's important during those times to ask myself what I need when I feel that way. It usually helps to remind myself that my needs are reasonable and valid and that there are people in my life who regularly embrace me and welcome my needs while I also embrace them and their needs. I reflect on my strengths and embrace the full range of emotions and realities that encompass my identity. God can handle my complex feelings, my intensity, my desires, and my hopes. And God embraces me as I am in my most successful and my most flawed moments. I speak honestly about my feelings, I pray and meditate, and I practice good self-care by eating enough and being active. Using even one of these tools leads me to a better spiritual and emotional place.

Self-awareness will help you lead with humility. You may find it helpful to assume the greatest lesson from the reading is for you. Make it clear that your journey of expanding self-awareness is ongoing. Sharing insight about your struggles often opens the door for others to share their doubts, fears, and obstacles. Remove the log in your own eye, and let others worry about their specks. (See Matthew 7:3.) Avoid spiritual comparisons and seek to celebrate each group member's value and successes.

Journaling briefly after each group may help increase your self-awareness. Ask yourself what went well, what moments seemed transformational, and what facilitated those moments. Reflect on what could have gone better for a few minutes while you clean up coffee mugs and snacks (if you're at home) or on your drive home from wherever you met. Ask yourself how you encountered others, God, and yourself. Were your encounters with others challenging, loving, friendly, or conflictual? Did you encounter God's presence, love, and comfort or feel a lack of guidance? Did tears or sadness unexpectedly bring up an encounter within yourself about family, money, or parenting? Focused reflection can enhance your self-awareness and help you grow as you continue to lead.

Rather than a project to be completed by a milestone birthday, self-awareness is an ongoing process that unfolds over years; there is always more to explore and learn about yourself. The human experience is an adventure with all kinds of unexpected twists and internal responses, and you do not need to fear it. Pay close attention to your thoughts, feelings, and interpersonal patterns. Spend time exploring what you feel and believe, and be open to changes. I am still learning, and I am sometimes surprised by what I learn when I pay close attention to feelings, relationships, and experiences that bring me joy.

After my book *Revealed* was published, a former client reached out to me. She said that she had not liked me as a group therapy leader at the eating disorders treatment center because she didn't think I could relate to what people with eating disorders were going through in meal groups. However, she went on to say that my vulnerability in sharing my history of an eating disorder in the book helped her understand how God was working through me in her life then and that God was continuing to work through me in her life through *Revealed*. Sharing openly for others' benefit had involved risk, uncertainty, and discomfort; but her response encouraged me to keep sharing even when it is difficult and vulnerable so that others can feel less alone and witness God's healing presence. Even though I held back initially in a professionally appropriate way, this experience showed me how others can make false assumptions or misunderstand us when we hold back from sharing openly.

Remember that the heroes of faith in biblical stories have their share of struggles too. Paul struggles with his unnamed thorn (see 2 Corinthians 12:7), David's wandering on a rooftop leads him to commit adultery and murder (see 2 Samuel 11), and Mary and Martha question Jesus' timing when he shows up after Lazarus dies (see John 11). Your group will benefit when you share some degree of vulnerability. Truthfully sharing your experience can be as important as sharing the truth of scripture.

Relationships communicate and demonstrate the truth of scripture. Without risk and honesty, connections remain shallow. Show up for your group as your authentic, delightfully fallible, and beautifully complex self. If it's been a difficult week, say so. Everyone has been hurt after taking a risk. Some people show themselves to be unworthy of trust and vulnerability, but those experiences help you make better judgments about who to open up to and how quickly to do so. As the group leader, you can create an environment that facilitates interpersonal risk-taking and safety from oversharing in a way that leads to spiritual and emotional depth.

Use emotional language to identify transformational moments in your group. Most emotions are iterations of sadness, anger, fear, or gladness. Use process comments to identify and respond to emotional cues in yourself and your group members. Remember that you can receive support from your group; you are there to participate in the transformational relationships, not just to support your group members. You can share your pleasant and unpleasant feelings and experiences with your group. Tell your group members when they are having a positive influence on you. I can still think of people who probably have no idea how much I enjoyed talking to them at a meeting, how much I needed a compliment they offered to me in a key moment, or how I resolved to model some aspect of my life after them. Vulnerability includes sharing your negative experiences as well, but be careful not to treat your group as a therapy group. If you find yourself bringing many emotional challenges to your group or doing most of the talking, seek emotional support in other ways so you can show up to your group ready to lead.

Many of us fear vulnerability because we think that once the floodgates open, the waves will overwhelm us and we will not be able to contain our disclosures. One of the most common concerns I hear from clients is the fear of burdening others with their emotional challenges. We all can worry about becoming a burden to others. What if we share more than we intend to? What will we do then? What if the resulting emotion becomes intolerable? While these questions are understandable, vulnerability can happen in manageable steps. Healthy vulnerability happens in the context of good self-care. Sharing and closeness happens in the most balanced and rewarding way when we are present for it and share a little bit at a time in a way that matches the quality and closeness of our relationships. When our judgment is impaired or we are coping in unhealthy ways, we are more likely to experience a vulnerability hangover from having shared too much. We all walk a continuum and seek a balance between sharing vulnerably in trusting relationships and guarding our hearts with healthy boundaries. When we get the balance right, our vulnerability leads to mutual closeness and caring. We generally feel honored when someone trusts us with a difficult truth.

Some tips for sharing wisely and maintaining balance include asking yourself the following questions:

1. Am I emotionally present and grounded? Come to the conversation in as relaxed and calm a state as possible. Take some deep breaths and notice the feel of the room. Make eye contact and note the sights, sounds, smells, and feelings in your environment.

2. How am I feeling? Identify an emotion. You don't have to understand, explain, or analyze why you are having the feeling in order to have it, share it, and benefit from the resulting connection.

3. Can I take an emotional risk? It is almost never as bad as you think it's going to be. When I'm feeling ambivalent about whether to share a vulnerable moment with someone and consider whether the risk is well-timed, I'm almost always relieved that I had the conversation.

4. Can this relationship support the discussion I want to have? What are the general attitudes of the people you are with, and what degree of time and effort has been spent building trust with them? If you're just getting to know the person or group, start small with your vulnerability. Sharing too much too quickly can set you up for regret or a vulnerability hangover. Well-established relationships can support more vulnerable discussions.

5. Am I doing this often enough in a balanced way? Sharing your emotions regularly is like maintaining a balanced eating plan. You have to fuel your body regularly to sustain the energy and concentration required for your day-to-day life. Without adequate connection in relationships, you may feel isolated and depleted. If you restrict food early in the day, you likely will eat more than you intend in the late afternoon and evening. When you lack steady sources of emotional support, you may end up excessively sharing in a context where it would have been better to take smaller steps first. Practice steady, intentional vulnerability so it does not come out all at once or at an inopportune time.

6. What will I actively disclose, and what am I ready to say if asked? Sometimes we initiate a discussion because we want to proactively enter into deeper vulnerability; other times we respond to someone who is asking us to open up more. Sometimes others push us to disclose more than we feel ready to share. One time at a dinner party, one of the guests found out Dusty had a degree in biblical studies. She immediately inquired about his thoughts on complex theological concepts like heaven and hell. He replied, "Let's talk about that the second time we meet."

7. What is my purpose in sharing? Consider whether sharing your heart in this instance builds up others and supports your values. You do not need to feel compelled to share every feeling you experience. Guard your heart when a relationship can't yet support the confrontation or expression of emotion. Hold back when doing so is good self-care. Maybe you need to work through an emotion or experience first in your journal or talk through it with a close friend or therapist. It's okay to give it some time, pray through it, and share when the time feels right and the relationship can support the conversation.

Sometimes you may worry about whether you have shared too much. Sometimes you may share more than you intended or more than was helpful. You and your group can still thrive. Remember that leading a group is not about being perfect. Stay engaged and communicate openly; be flexible and learn as you move forward. Embrace awkwardness! Everyone experiences it. It's never too late to revisit and process an experience if you're having difficulty letting it go: "I'm aware that I shared a lot about my personal struggles last week. I'm worried it may have been too much. I want to check in with you all about how you experienced it."

Some of the most powerfully vulnerable sharing occurs when people are willing to share their impressions and feelings about one another in the present moment. It's possible for a person to share all kinds of details about experiences in the past without really connecting to you. It's also possible for someone to share relatively little content about their life but share openly with you about how they experience you in the moment, and a powerful connection can result. As a group leader, focus on what you're noticing and feeling in the moment and try putting it into words.

Assess how you're doing as you enter your small-group meeting each week. On a scale of 1–10, how present and grounded are you? Have you experienced balance in your sleeping, eating, working, resting, and general life routines? Engage in the ongoing process of knowing yourself, make adjustments as needed, and share yourself wisely in ways that match the relationships in the group.

Leader Checklist for Knowing and Sharing Yourself

✓ Courageously share your less-than-perfect self so that group members feel free to share their perspectives and experiences too. Pursue self-awareness through your own study, therapy, journaling, spiritual direction, or personality inventories.

✓ Assume that the greatest lesson in the reading is for you.

✓ Share enough to convey that you're human and have struggles like anyone else.

✓ Remember that the heroes of Bible stories struggled with the complexity of the human experience just like you do.

✓ Use emotional language and process comments to encourage a focus on the powerful, moment-to-moment experience in the group that transforms its members.

✓ Seek a balance between sharing vulnerably in trusting relationships and guarding your heart with healthy boundaries.

✓ Ask yourself the seven questions in this chapter as a guide for discerning whether the timing feels right to share your feelings and perspectives.

STRATEGY 6
Deal with Problems

God is our refuge and strength, a very present help in trouble.

—PSALM 46:1

Problem dynamics occur when our particular distortions, lack of clarity, and misunderstandings come into conflict with those of another person. When problem patterns arise in relationships among group members, the group may struggle. We all bring some type of potential problem dynamics to a group. Relationships develop based on current and past dynamics. When problematic communication patterns arise, we can respond in loving and effective ways with a few simple strategies. Love and maturity can thrive if we deal with problem dynamics in a constructive way.

The following are some common problem dynamics I've observed while leading small groups and therapy groups. Group members will look to you as the leader to notice and do something about these dynamics when they arise. The sooner you address the problem, the better. If you're noticing a problem dynamic, chances are great that others are too. Group members may become anxious or shut down, and the group may fail to thrive. With each common problem scenario, I've offered some specific ideas about how to avoid the dynamic, statements you can use to help shift the dynamic while valuing all group members, or ways to steer the group toward creating a healthier dynamic.

The idealized leader. The group sees the leader as faultless and seeks to become exactly like the leader. This dynamic diminishes or overlooks valuable individual differences in favor of one personality style and perspective. Group members conform to one another and seek to please the leader rather than focus on genuine spiritual growth. The risk for groupthink increases. To avoid this dynamic, be sure to share ways that you struggle with the topics being discussed and remain mindful of your own challenges.

The turn-taking dynamic. The group develops a pattern where each person responds in turn to each question the leader asks. Group meetings look like a series of one-on-one conversations between the leader and each group member rather than a robust and spontaneous discussion involving the group as a whole. As the leader, seek to facilitate more spontaneous interaction by being willing to sit with a few moments of silence. Let another group member respond rather than making a comment. The group should be less a series of interactions with the leader and more a series of interactions between each person and each other person, dynamic and coming to life as the living system it is.

The monopolizing member. One group member does most of the talking and communicates their thoughts in a monologue style rather than as part of an interactive conversation. Other members find it difficult to voice their perspectives.[1] On the one hand, a high degree of participation in a group has a positive impact on the person's derived benefit. On the other hand, an imbalance can disrupt the group process and keep the group from reaching its potential. If one or two people talk most of the time, carrying all the weight of the group discussion, they may feel compelled to help facilitate, be uncomfortable with silence, or just like having space to assert their opinions. Often those who are afraid they are talking too much are not the people who need to change their behaviors. Monopolizing members tend to lack the self-awareness to realize they are dominating the discussion. They may not be receptive to feedback or pick up on the social cues that indicate others' discomfort with their excessive comments. When one person is the default talker, others may check out or disengage, which may leave them only a short step away from deciding not to attend the group at all. Try to gently direct discussion to include other group members. Ask what others in the group think about the topic being discussed. Some tangents are okay, but if a monopolizing member's story gets lengthy or feels too tangential, look for an opportunity to connect the story back to the topic for the evening.

Attendance problems/group dropouts. When a group member bows out, your group may have less varied perspectives and an increased possibility that others will soon follow. If someone leaves the group, try to avoid saying, "That's okay! No problem!" and instead invite the person to say more about their decision to leave. You do not need to convince them to stay, but opening the conversation may be a valuable opportunity for the person to define for themselves why they've chosen to leave and for you to learn whether you need to change something in the group. A group member's decision to leave is out of your control and is not a failure on your part. If someone doesn't want to be there, your group dynamic may even improve. You can use this response if a group member decides to leave: "I'll miss having you in the group, but I respect your decision. Thanks for talking to me about it."

Spiritual competition. Unproductive competition and comparisons can lead to jealousy and distract from the purpose of the group. Small groups are not a contest for the title of Most Devout Christian. Your verbal affirmation of every member's specific strengths or insights will go a long way. Whenever someone is speaking about others who are not in the room, try to steer the discussion back to the people who are in the room. "What a tough situation she's going through. What came up for you when you heard about her struggle?" You can discourage a competitive dynamic through humor and an intentional effort not to participate in unhealthy competition. Normalize struggles and imperfection with statements like, "I find it hard to motivate myself to pray" or "I felt mad at God this week."

Excessive silence. Some people process thoughts and feelings internally rather than talking through them. While these group members may be silent during a majority of the group time, they may be very engaged in thought and walk away with significant insights and benefits. Silence does not always mean something is wrong, but it may leave us curious about whether the quiet person is angry, offended, or depressed. Be sure to notice if a typically talkative person becomes atypically, abruptly withdrawn one week. Regularly check in on quieter members. These internal processors likely prefer that you check in one-on-one rather than in front of the group.

Confusing nonverbals. Our nonverbal behavior tends to be more truthful than our words. Sometimes a person's nonverbal behavior is difficult to interpret. Inappropriate laughter, a complete absence of eye contact, or unexpected tears can present a challenge to leaders. These behaviors are part of human communication, and you do not need to evaluate every instance. However, if certain behaviors arise as patterns, you can use some tools to help your group stay on course with your stated goals. When a nonverbal behavior is difficult to interpret, use process comments to bring clarity to the room.[2] Try to maintain a tone of curiosity rather than judgment as you address your concern: "You seem sad right now; what prompted your tears? Do you want to say any more about what's coming up for you?" Or start with and speak about your own feelings: "I'm struggling to understand your reaction; can you say more about it?"

Chronic complaining and negativity. Help-rejecting patterns and complaining can suck the life out of a group. Such behaviors can pull you to feel anxious and to solve the person's problem for them. Try to resist being pulled into a miserable and repetitive exchange where you over-function and offer suggestion after suggestion while the group member meets every suggestion with "Yes, but . . ." or "I've already done that, and it didn't work." Try to put some responsibility back on that person. Lead with empathy, and empower them to address their dilemma: "That sounds so stressful. I would really be discouraged too. What do you think your next step needs to be in moving through this?" If the negativity is directed toward others, ask about the complainer's direct experience as quickly as possible: "Have you ever dealt with something like that? If so, how did you handle it?"

A difficult personality. Some people have long-standing, complex personality dynamics that are resistant to change. These group members need love and belonging as much as anyone, but you should not allow more challenging group members to undermine or hijack the whole group. One of the most challenging personality styles involves a dramatic, all-or-nothing presentation of constant crisis along with a pull to be rescued. Try to balance empathy with healthy boundaries and facilitate the person getting additional support outside of the group.

If any of these problem dynamics arise, you can address them with a balance of clarity and directness and kindness and love. Jesus offered us the example of addressing others clearly and directly throughout his life. If you feel like your group is veering off course from the central focus and purpose you established together, a problem dynamic may be arising. Address the issue as directly as you can and as soon as you can. Use these tools or seek guidance from experienced leaders to help guide you back to a healthy and transformational group dynamic.

Leader Checklist for Dealing with Problems

✓ Identify common problem patterns such as idealizing the leader, turn-taking, monopolizing, absences and drop-outs, competition, excessive silence, confusing nonverbals, negativity, and challenging personality dynamics.

✓ Address problem dynamics as soon as you can by gently redirecting, returning to the purpose of the group, and keeping adequate structure and boundaries in place.

✓ It's your role as leader to address problem dynamics but not to fix members' problems. Ask for guidance from an experienced leader and consider whether you need to refer a group member to other supports.

STRATEGY 7
Make Space

Now I know only in part; then I will know fully, even as I have been fully known.

—1 CORINTHIANS 13:12

As group leaders we walk the line between confidence and uncertainty. We long to know and understand, to be known and understood. Part of our purpose in a group is to learn. But no matter how much we come to understand about the Bible, about ourselves, and about other people, we can be sure that there will still be a degree of uncertainty that we must learn to tolerate in our faith journeys. Our hearts echo a familiar response to Jesus: "I believe; help my unbelief" (Mark 9:24). Groups offer transformational relationships that can usher us into an experience of knowing more and being more fully known. Knowing one another and knowing God includes making sense together of what to do with our uncertainty and differing perspectives. Our task as leaders is to make space for uncertainty, for silence, and for everyone in the group to speak. This task begins with the courage and humility to enter into our own uncertainty. We can be confidently uncertain and own the fact that we do not have all the answers or see as God sees. It can take tremendous pressure off us as leaders. A young woman I know recently met with a well-known author and spiritual leader. What struck her most about the seasoned leader was her willingness to be wrong, ask questions, and change her mind. If we believe we have the answers to life's most difficult questions, we begin to tread on God's territory and have lost sight of our need for God's help and guidance. In contrast, when we embrace humility and limitations and learn to keep asking questions and living within our limits, we can engage in beautiful encounters where we embrace new perspectives and sit with difficult questions without the urgency to reach solutions. At the same time, solutions will emerge when we come together in humility, looking to the Spirit as our group facilitator. In his Gospel, John writes that the Spirit will guide us into all the truth. (See John 16:13.) Though we have partial knowledge, we have a trustworthy guide.

Regardless of our leadership training, experience, and insight, we do not know another person's experience and do not have perfect ability to interpret scripture. But we can still lead well. We benefit from asking ourselves where our value and worth lies: in having answers, appearing knowledgeable and competent, and getting the whole group's approval? Or can we rest securely in Christ, knowing that we are already good enough? Can we tolerate partial clarity and trust in the Spirit's timing and guidance? In the book of Ecclesiastes, the Teacher shares the futility of wisdom: "I applied my mind to know wisdom and to know madness and folly. I perceived that this also is but a chasing after wind. For in much wisdom is much vexation, and those who increase knowledge increase sorrow" (Eccles. 1:17-18).

Ironically, the more I accept how far I have to go spiritually along with the vast difference between my understanding of God and the actual identity of God, the more I can relax into my confidence as a leader. Leading is not about answers; it is about facilitating relationships and moving toward a common spiritual goal. In a small group, I believe it's a greater spiritual pursuit to be all-loving than all-knowing.

Release yourself from the pressure to have all the answers, since no one does. Open yourself instead to the relationships available to you in your small group. Every person invites you into a new understanding of some aspect of the body of Christ that no one else can reflect in quite the same way. You will guide your group toward clarity as you ask questions, share experiences, and go to the Bible and other resources together in a joint search for truth. Spiritual growth occurs when your group asks and sits with difficult questions without feeling pressured to rush to an answer. Facilitate an environment where difficult questions are welcome. Here are some options for what to say and do when you do not know what to say in a group meeting:

I don't know. Just say it and own it. You don't know everything and will look insecure or lose respect by acting like you know things you don't.

That's a great question, and I need to sit with it for a while. Does anyone else have a response? Do not pressure yourself to be the one who offers insight. A group member who is quietly absorbing the discussion may have something wise and insightful to say. Crowding out other voices in the room does a disservice to your group.

Let's figure this out together. Who knows a scripture passage or has an experience or insight relevant to this question? Even if you don't come to a solution or answer to the question, you may gain some insight or a new perspective or turn to an interesting discussion. You can assume some desire among the group to collaborate and examine the Bible together. You can assume some willingness among your group to pursue wisdom in the scriptures and in the group's collective wisdom.

I've wrestled with that same question myself. This brings the question back to something (or, rather, someone) you do know— you. Speak about other related questions, any perspectives you have, and listen for others' insights that emerge during the discussion. In one small group, a member of our group asked, "How do I know whether I'm sensing a prompt from God or it's just my own thoughts and feelings?" While I cannot possibly know the answer to this, I could speak about the times when I have asked the same question and have erred on the side of acting on positive, generous, peaceful behavior that is consistent with what I understand about God's nature and will.

I'd like to find out too. How can we get closer to understanding it? Remember that you can be confident, capable, and lead effectively without having answers for everyone. Your group will value your willingness to engage with them meaningfully. You can create space where group members feel secure enough in the group to voice a variety of perspectives that may or may not be spiritually sound or perfectly on point. In this type of space, group members will grow in faith.

Make space for silence. While excessive silence can be a problem, some silence is a gift to your group. When something important weighs on group members, they tend to sit with some ambivalence about whether to voice their thoughts. Leaving room for an occasional (possibly uncomfortable) silence can create an opening for the group to go deeper as individuals share vulnerable thoughts or reactions to the topic. Group members may need those extra few seconds to muster the willingness or courage to say something that could be transformational for the person's relationships within the group, with God, or with themselves.

When you create space for silence, group members may step in right away to fill the silence out of their own discomfort or anxiety, especially if they have a tendency to rescue others from discomfort. Notice group members' nonverbal reactions when you try to allow silence. You may notice that certain people appear to be engaged and thinking deeply as the more verbal members of the group speak up. You can create openings for the quieter, more introverted members to speak even if your attempts to create silence fail. As you begin to identify which members are quieter, think about ways you can direct the conversation toward contributions from quieter members as you prepare for each group meeting. For example, you might engage an introverted member by saying, "You've had experience as a social worker; what do you think about this topic?"

Make space for group members to sit with their struggles and problems. If you have a rescuer in the group who keeps jumping in to fill silence or offer solutions, you may decide to address it one-on-one with the person outside of group time and appeal to the rescuer's strengths and desire to help: "I notice you're a natural helper, and your compassion is a gift to the group. I've been wondering if you'd help me with something. I think there are others in the group who may benefit from a chance to think through tough questions and sit with some of the discomfort of not knowing so they can work it out in their own timing. Will you help me create space for them to sit with some silence and encourage their comments and involvement?" Note how the group member receives your feedback. Many people receive feedback well and adjust. Others profusely apologize. Some may seem fine with the feedback but will feel resentful, and it will come out in passive-aggressive ways. Others will not hear it or will become defensive. Others feel wounded and cry. Offer feedback one-on-one when possible, and clearly state the behavior changes you are requesting. Rescuers may have strong leadership qualities; invite them to help you create space for other group members to participate and grow.

Leader Checklist for Making Space

✓ Learn to tolerate a degree of uncertainty in your faith journey.

✓ Make space in your group for uncertainty, silence, and every group member's voice.

✓ Remember that leading is less about answers and more about facilitating relationships.

✓ Allow the Spirit to be your guide in moving toward the group's common spiritual goals.

✓ Welcome difficult topics and questions, and know that "I don't know" is a valid response.

✓ Invite quiet members into the discussion, and invite talkative members into your efforts to create space for everyone to grow.

STRATEGY 8
End Well

*For everything there is a season, and a time for every matter
under heaven: . . . a time to weep, and a time to laugh; a
time to mourn, and a time to dance.*

—ECCLESIASTES 3:1, 4

I ran into a fellow group leader in the neighborhood salon
one day. We started chatting about our small groups, and she
leaned in and asked, almost apologetically, "Is it okay to end
our group?"

"Of course," I encouraged her. It is okay to end a group. If
well-timed and done with thought and care, a group can end
well and relationships built in the group can continue thriving.

It's a good idea to discuss an estimated time line for the
life of the group at the beginning. Doing so creates a healthy
boundary from day one because everyone knows the scope of
the commitment. The end of the group will not come as a sur-
prise. If you choose to leave the group open-ended, make space
from time to time for the group to have an open discussion
where you can assess members' attendance and energy, your
balance between the group and other commitments, how the

group is going, and how everyone is feeling about continuing the group for another season.

When you've determined that the group is approaching an ending, create opportunities over the last few weeks or months for people to voice how they feel about the group ending and express any unresolved feelings or unfinished discussions that they need to address so that they can feel a sense of closure. Endings can bring up past grief experiences, and your group will need an opportunity to acknowledge what the group has meant to them and what they will take with them from the group experience. Just as you set a tone in the beginning of the group, you can model how to end well by creating space for discussion, acknowledging your own feelings about the group's ending, and instilling hope that the relationships built in the group can continue.

Meaningful relationships forged through weekly prayer and Bible study over an extended length of time create a connection that allows the relationships to continue outside the structure of the group. Existing relationships often transform through the shared tears, prayer requests, and theological conversations a small group offers. Groups need to end, but the transformational relationships can continue in other ways.

One small group Dusty and I led lasted for about two years. Years later, when one of our group members was declining during her battle with late-stage cancer, we gathered for a group reunion. In December 2017 our friend Steve sent an email asking if we could reconnect to pray for his wife, Sabina. Sabina had come to a point of some key decisions in her breast cancer treatment. She and Steve were making difficult decisions and they needed prayer, so they turned to our small group. In the years since we met as a group, we had scattered to various cities and churches and moved on in our lives. Some of us were still nearby. One couple had moved to Australia, and another had moved to the suburbs of Atlanta (which feel as far away from the city as Australia). But for an evening during a busy December, we gathered and reconvened for prayer and Skyped in the couple in Australia. I rested my hand on Sabina's knee and prayed aloud, wondering silently if this would be the last time I would sit with her, feel her warmth, and see her hopeful smile. It would be. We reminisced and exchanged white elephant gifts. Sabina wore a radiant smile and, other than some trouble walking and the use of a cane, she seemed herself. She was tuned in to everyone around her, laughing and affectionate.

Something about our weekly connection over snacks and coffee striving together to understand the Bible had forged a bond that stayed firm over years. That bond resurfaced powerfully as the glue that would hold the members of our group together for a few moments. We knew how to pray for one another, and our styles of prayer and coping were the same as they'd always been. The individual nuances of our prayers were a familiar comfort during an unfamiliar, tragic sadness. The prospect of death lingered and hung in the same air as our prayers, but faith and love lived on among us.

What could I pray for in that moment? For life, health, a miracle? Did I share Sabina's faith that she was simply facing a trial from which she would emerge any day, miraculously healed? My skepticism, fear, and lack of faith lingered beneath my words, as science and statistics about cancer reverberated through my mind. I prayed with a calm, practiced voice, but I believed I was asking God for the impossible. Despite my conflicted feelings, hope remained. My hope came from knowing that the connection we felt in that moment was real and sustaining.

A year later I sat between Dusty and a friend from that group as another group member stood behind a lectern and read her moving memorial letter to Sabina. She had walked closely with Sabina during her final months and stood tearful but strong as she offered a tribute to the friend she knew well. Their relationship began in our small group. Though it ended painfully, the richness both women experienced through each other's friendship clearly transcended the pain and rested securely in the memories and feelings shared with the tearful mourners that day.

Meetings and groups end, and relationships change and evolve. Grief is disturbingly real, but you and your group members can trudge through its uncertain course side-by-side. When one group ends, the possibilities for a new group begin. Relationships can continue even if they look different than they have during the course of the group. Members will continue to process and work out conversations and dynamics from the group experience long after the group ends. The group is a microcosm, and group members can take what they've learned from one another into the groups they may now be equipped to lead, the larger congregation, and the community. The transformation and spiritual maturity that occurs in groups has far-reaching effects. You can end well.

Leader Checklist for Ending Well

✓ The end of a group does not mean the failure of a group.

✓ Give yourself permission to end the group at an agreed-upon time, and communicate openly about the ending.

✓ In open-ended groups, periodically check in regarding group members' feelings about continuing the group for another season.

✓ Make space for group members to grieve the group's ending.

✓ The transformational relationships created or evolved in a group can continue beyond the end of the group.

CONCLUSION

Recently I led a retreat on the destigmatization of mental illness. Some of the sessions included active Taekwondo-related movement. I could see how the two were related, but I received pushback that it did not seem to fit into the theme of the retreat. When I learned that some attendees felt they didn't have enough time in small-group discussions, I worked with the church leaders to cut some of my prepared program and instead led a large group discussion about mental illness. Many individuals shared their encounters with mental illness, and at the end of the session we all broke boards to symbolize breaking through the obstacles that we face. The energy in the room was incredible.

I am proud of the way we collaborated to honor the program I'd prepared while responding to the collective wisdom of the group. In the end, participants shared that it was one of the best retreats in years, and I could not have created it within my isolated efforts to craft the perfect program. As you know and share yourself as a leader, people will respond in a variety of ways. Know that God created you in love and that you have a valuable perspective. Have a plan for your group, but receive feedback non-defensively and allow your plan to be adjusted by your collective wisdom as you move forward.

With the knowledge about how groups function and the practically useful tools and examples you've learned, you can lead effectively knowing that you do not need to lead perfectly. Use the checklists to help you put into practice what you've learned. The hardest part of leading a group is being willing to enter into the uncomfortable spaces of vulnerability and self-awareness and to search for collective wisdom. But the rewards are great. Your efforts to be an effective leader will make a difference to your group.

Much of what I say in this book is easy enough to understand, but it is far more difficult to implement consistently. My prescription in this book is to know and share yourself and to show up without need for answers and neatly arranged solutions. But everyone, including myself, can have powerful tendencies to pull back, to shy away from vulnerability, to maintain some distance when life begins to feel too full, complicated, or messy. As I explore unexpected turns in my evolving faith and rely on a large calendar and my neighbors to support my children's school and activities, I am navigating the tension between seeking self-sufficient autonomy and needing other people. I'm out of my comfort zone.

Sometimes I pull back from my small groups, and other times I move into deeper involvement with them. Some groups are brief, and others go on for years. I revisit my values of integrity and compassion as a guide and remain open to where God is leading me. As your small groups progress through stages and deeper levels of process, you may hesitate to engage, may pull back, or may invest more. Revisit your values and pay close attention to what you learn from all the small groups in your life. Let your values guide your choices, and you will continue to learn what you need to know on your faith journey.

During times of transition, my internal wisdom points me back toward the collective wisdom of the groups in my life. During a recent break from one of my small groups, I deepened relationships during a weekend trip with four friends. I auditioned and joined the cast of my church's production of *Peter Pan*. I sought connections with my Taekwondo companions and with my neighbors and colleagues. These groups draw me into belonging, and I can sense their transformational potential.

In the final scene of *Peter Pan*, I stand onstage as the now grown-up Wendy. Peter returns through the nursery window, expecting Wendy to fly away with him and return to Neverland for spring cleaning. I exclaim onstage, "I can't come. I've forgotten how to fly . . . I grew up a long time ago." I bring the emotion from my own experiences into the moment, and I connect with Peter Pan and Jane, my character's daughter. In that moment I am deeply connected to myself and other people.

The play rehearsals and performances facilitate the power of being part of a group. Carlson, Caleb, and Zach play Lost Boys. Dusty, our friends, and our extended family support us in the audience. Director Bob works tirelessly to bring it all together with three separate casts of children. Everyone plays a part, and the collective effort results in a beautiful outcome. We are not just the moviegoers; we are the movie. We play roles and interact with one another within a powerful dynamic that facilitates emotional and spiritual transformation.

Your group will thrive with the same pulse of collective effort and an outcome that transcends what an individual person can do while transforming every individual in it. Every group member plays a part in the life, plot, action, and resolution of the group, and you can facilitate the process. Play your part well using what you've learned in this book. Empower others to play their parts well too. Practice your faith. Focus, stretch, and listen deeply.

I am hopeful that amid painful debates and divisions among Christians, the transformational experiences of small groups can create a ripple effect felt by the larger church and our communities. As small groups embrace and value critical thinking, vulnerability, and self-awareness and find a balance between structure and flexibility, we can thrive. We can know and share ourselves, deal with problems, and make space. When relationships or groups find their end, they can end well.

Bonds forged between those who differ from one another help create a healthier and more whole body of Christ. Start with your small group, and offer healing messages: You're enough. You're not too much. You're embraced as you are. You also can do better, and we will help equip you so you don't have to forge the path in isolation. You can let down your guard. You can be who you are—all of who you are—and be valued in the body of Christ.

I know I will continue to thrive in my small groups, driven by love and a willingness to embrace more questions than answers. I will keep showing up, and when called to lead, I will lead well. So will you.

NOTES

Introduction

1. As a discipleship and groups coordinator at our church for two years, I often received requests from group leaders for "a study that is biblically based and goes deeper than the typical book or study." There are many excellent studies out there, but I saw a need for something else that fit that description, so I wrote a study that is exactly that: a look at Bible stories, viewed through the lens of a psychologist, that will challenge you and take you deeper in your journey of healing and maturity in your faith. See *Revealed: What the Bible Can Teach You About Yourself*, which includes a thorough facilitator guide. For an additional selection of quality studies, check out the Upper Room Bookstore. If you are looking for a Bible with notes in the text, I'd recommend the NRSV Study Bible published by HarperCollins. There are also great websites for locating passages in the Bible with particular words or topics (www.biblegateway.org) and for studying a passage more in-depth based on a calendar rotation through the Bible followed by many churches called the lectionary (www.textweek.org).

Section 1

Enter the System

1. Donelson R. Forsyth, *Group Dynamics*, 3rd ed. (Belmont, CA: Wadsworth Publishing Company, 1999), 15.

Navigate the Stages

1. Donelson R. Forsyth, *Group Dynamics*, 3rd ed. (Belmont, CA: Wadsworth Publishing Company, 1999), 15.
2. Irvin D. Yalom, *The Theory and Practice of Group Psychotherapy*, 5th ed. (New York: Basic Books, 2005), 292.
3. Donelson R. Forsyth, *Group Dynamics*, 3rd ed. (Belmont, CA: Wadsworth Publishing Company, 1999), 330–31.

Seek Transformation

1. Debbara Dingman, conversation in therapy, 2005.
2. Linda Buchanan, conversation in supervision, 2006.

Become a Transformational Group

1. Irvin D. Yalom, *The Theory and Practice of Group Psychotherapy*, 5th ed. (New York: Basic Books, 2005), 1–2.
2. Irvin D. Yalom, *The Theory and Practice of Group Psychotherapy*, 5th ed. (New York: Basic Books, 2005), 7.
3. Michael Casey, *Sacred Reading: The Ancient Art of* Lectio Divina (Liguori, MO: Liguori/Triumph, 1995), 79.

Section 2

Practice Faith

1. *The Upper Room Disciplines: A Book of Daily Devotions 2019* (Nashville, TN: Upper Room Books, 2018).
2. Kristen E. Vincent, *A Bead and a Prayer: A Beginner's Guide to Protestant Prayer Beads* (Nashville, TN: Upper Room Books, 2013).
3. J. Dana Trent, *One Breath at a Time: A Skeptic's Guide to Christian Meditation* (Nashville, TN: Upper Room Books, 2019).

Focus

1. Brené Brown, *Dare to Lead: Brave Work. Tough Conversations. Whole Hearts* (New York: Random House, 2018), 188–89.

Stretch but Not Too Far

1. Irvin D. Yalom, *The Theory and Practice of Group Psychotherapy*, 5th ed. (New York: Basic Books, 2005), 129.

Know and Share Yourself

1. Angela D. Schaffner, *Revealed: What the Bible Can Teach You About Yourself* (Nashville, TN: Upper Room Books, 2019).
2. Don Richard Riso and Russ Hudson, *The Wisdom of the Enneagram: The Complete Guide to Psychological and Spiritual Growth for the Nine Personality Types* (New York: Bantam Books, 1999), 11–12.
3. Tom Rath, *StrengthsFinder 2.0* (New York: Gallup Press, 2007).
4. Jennifer V. Fayard, "Five Big Reasons to Embrace the Big Five Personality Traits," *Psychology Today* (blog), October 17, 2019, https://www.psychologytoday.com/us/blog/people-are-strange/201910/five-big-reasons-embrace-the-big-five-personality-traits.

Deal with Problems

1. Irvin D. Yalom, *The Theory and Practice of Group Psychotherapy*, 5th ed. (New York: Basic Books, 2005), 391–92, 397–98.
2. Marianne Schneider Corey and Gerald Corey, *Groups: Process and Practice*, 5th ed. (Pacific Grove, CA: Brooks/Cole Publishing Company, 1997), 143.

/